Echoes From the Nine Foot Road

An Autobiography

A Personal History of Gospel Preaching and Issues of
Concern From 1945 – 2009

Connie W. Adams

ISBN 10: 1-58427-270-8

ISBN 13: 978-158427-270-0

Guardian of Truth Foundation
P.O. Box 9670
Bowling Green, Kentucky 42102
1-800-428-0121
www.truthbooks.net

Table of Contents

Dedication

This book is dedicated to the two women who have stood beside me in the preaching of the gospel. Both of them have been devoted to the Lord and to me. Without their help, I could not have done the work which the Lord has allowed me to do.

To **Bobbie 1** who was called away after thirty-five years of marriage

and

To **Bobby 2** who has been my loving companion for twenty-three years and counting,

this book is dedicated.

Connie W. Adams (1930-)

By Way of Introduction

For a number of years, friends and family members have urged me to write this book. I have delayed until now partly because I did not want to be thought presumptuous or vain or on some sort of ego trip. Over the years, while visiting in many homes during meetings, some incident would be related, either humorous or historical, and someone would say, "You ought to write a book." My life and work have brought me into contact with a number of interesting people who have had, in one way or another, a marked influence on the Lord's work for over sixty years.

The final impetus which brought this to fruition was the encouragement of my wife, Bobby, and the urging of my longtime friend, Ron Halbrook, along with the men who shepherd the Lord's flock which meets on Hebron Lane, near Shepherdsville, Kentucky: Tom Brown, John Smith, and Laymon Byers. It is our good fortune to worship and work under their oversight. They urged me to block out time during the winter of 2008 and 2009 to complete the writing of this book.

I am deeply indebted to my wife, Bobby, for the many hours she has invested in entering all of this in the computer. Without her encouragement and help, this work would not have been done. Her careful proofing has also been of great value.

This book would not be in your hands were it not for the excellent editorial work of Mike Willis. Now, if the reader does not like this book, you have some idea as to where to place the blame. But it is sent forth in the hope that it will shed some light on the history of the Lord's work in the last sixty plus years as viewed from the vantage point of my own experience in it, and that the personal references will bring a smile, or perhaps a tear, as you relive with me the experiences of these years.

Connie W. Adams

Foreword
Wilson Adams

"I am not worthy to walk in his shadow. . . ." He probably doesn't remember saying that to me, but it etched in my mind like a river cuts through a canyon. It was 1986 and I stood with my father in Hopewell, Virginia and viewed one final time the lifeless remains of his father—Joyner Wilson Adams. "Granddaddy" never had much money or the advantages of higher education, but he had something better—he had integrity, knew the merits of hard work, and understood family devotion. Here was a man who wanted to preach the gospel and did so through a legacy that few can match. All three of his children were faithful Christians. His two sons became gospel preachers and his daughter married one. All nine grandchildren are Christians and three of them are gospel preachers and one married one. One of his grandsons is an elder in the church. J. W. Adams was a simple man from North Carolina who migrated to Virginia, married, and raised a godly family in the toughest of times.

This is the story of one of his sons.

From a humble (and humorous!) beginning of preaching along the Nine Foot Road near Newport, North Carolina, Connie W. Adams embarked upon a lifetime of gospel work that would span the next sixty plus years. From growing up along the Appomattox River in the heart of the Great Depression, the author relates to the hardship of that era, both culturally and religiously, while pointing to those who influenced him in the direction his life would take. Candid and penetrating, it is written in the context of a historical period that many fail to grasp. While professional historians have sought to capture the Twentieth Century among churches of Christ from an academic perspective, Adams offers the insight of one who came of age at the dawn of the last half-century. His life is a connection to the past and to a generation that has left us and of a generation that is all-too-quickly following one another into eternity.

I have known Connie W. Adams all fifty-one years of my life. While others could have been chosen to write these words, he chose me. I am honored. I am biased. I am his son.

Named after the Philadelphia Athletic legendary manager, Connie Mack (who managed and won more baseball games than any manager in major league history), Connie Adams anticipated a career in show business. Adams, his older brother Wiley, and an eastern Kentucky fiddle player named Weldon Warnock, literally played their way through college. Opening for such acts as Marty Robbins, Ray Price, and Kitty Wells, the Dixie Boys were thought to be on the road to Nashville and country music success. Except that all three had a love for something more important than music—they had decided to harmonize in proclaiming the precious strains of the gospel of Christ.

I don't think any of us realize how good they were or what a temptation they faced. Whether or not they would have met with success in the music industry is a moot point. What is known, however, are the many lives of those they touched because of a much higher endeavor.

One of my fondest memories of childhood is of my Dad's Sunday morning routine. Dressed and ready a half hour before anyone else, my brother and I would hear him plug in the black amplifier to his Gretsch guitar, and listen to him sing and pick his favorites. It was his way of relaxing prior to preaching and he still does it today. He has a new mandolin now and that, plus his guitar and fiddle, allows him to "pick and grin" whenever he can. Neither my brother nor I got the gene.

Dad worked hard and still does. People ask me his response when we ask him about retiring. I don't know because I'm smart enough not to ask. He will retire when the Lord calls him home and, if I know him, not a day sooner. Connie W. Adams loves God, loves the Book of God, and loves preaching the gospel as much as any man I have ever known. It is the fire within his bones.

He is not without his idiosyncrasies. He loves to wear a Stetson hat and cowboy boots. Always has. Once, while watching Porter Waggoner on the Grand Ole' Opry, he said to my mom, "I believe that is the ugliest man I ever saw." The next day Dad went down to the barbershop decked out in his cowboy attire when he noticed the curious stare of a stranger waiting his turn. When Dad stepped out of the chair and retrieved his Stetson, the fellow spoke, "Say," he said, "You wouldn't happen to be Porter Waggoner, would you?" To this day Weldon Warnock cannot tell that story but that he laughs himself into tears.

My Dad loves horses and the call of the American West. He and Bobby have a favorite ranch they frequent whenever travels take them anywhere close to Wyoming. But even that does not compare to his love for the Bluegrass state of Kentucky. Don't bother calling the house when his Kentucky Wildcats are on the hardwood—you will get a busy signal because he takes the phone off the hook. And it doesn't bother him at all to wear his Kentucky blue across the country or even to places like University Hall in Bloomington when Indiana friends offer tickets.

Echoes From the Nine Foot Road, above all, will help you understand religious thinking over the past sixty years. It will cause you to rethink the naïve mindset that says, "The division [institutionalism and the sponsoring church controversy] could have been averted had brethren been sweet and kind to each other." Adams' search for truth mirrored the search that many took during those years. My generation owes a debt of gratitude for the conviction and courage of those who stood for truth when it cost a lot to do so.

It will be impossible for you to read the sections about preaching overseas without feeling the heartbeat of Connie Adams. His desire to take the gospel to "all the nations" continues to this day. Even now when he talks of preaching in foreign lands, he cannot do so without weeping. He believes "the gospel is for all" and has lived it. And he minces no words when it comes to his disdain for shallow sermons and weak preaching. He is a preacher of the Book and calls all of us back to the only Book that counts.

His story of "the only Connie married to two 'Bobbie's'" (or Bobby) has made for some humorous anecdotes. My mother, "Bobbie," was one of a kind. But so is this "Bobby." "Mamaw," as our children call her, has reached out to love each child with a special affection, just like he has done for her grandchildren. I will never forget going with my father to meet his "date" at the Hyatt Regency restaurant in downtown Louisville. When I noted, "Since when do you go to the Hyatt for lunch?" he responded, "It's the only place where we won't run into anyone we know!" He was right. And, later, when I performed their wedding ceremony and spoke on "The Seasons of Life," I thought of how few and fortunate are those who are able to survive the blast of winter's death only to find spring again. I encouraged my Dad to marry again. We couldn't have been happier for both of them.

The hardest undertaking in life is to follow in your father's steps when he has been successful at his life's endeavor. I think of athletes or entertainers who have done that and I will tell you from personal experience that it is very hard and borders the impossible. It is hard because of the constant comparisons by people and the raising of the bar so high that you cannot possibly reach it. It isn't our father's fault, but it is factual nonetheless. It is one of the reasons my brother went in another direction—aviation. I can't blame him. He serves in a different way than either of us, for he serves as a shepherd of God's people. I decided to preach, however, and while most have been kind, some have put undue pressure on me to "be just like your dad."

In many ways I am. In other ways I am not. We may do the same work but we do it in our own way and style. He has friends with whom he is close, but so do I. And they aren't always the same. While we haven't always agreed on every matter of judgment, each respects the other for his convictions. Thus, to the oft-asked query, "How do you and your dad get along?" The answer—"Very well."

Our youngest son, Luke, and I drove to Pulaski, Tennessee last year to hear Dad in a meeting. The opportunity doesn't happen often but, when it does, it is special. That particular night, Dad preached on "Authority" and used a Power-Point chart. Luke was amazed and laughed all the way home that his "Papaw" is more technologically savvy than am I. It was a humbling experience.

I found the memories of his years as editor of *Searching the Scriptures* to be nostalgic and, at the same time, oddly predictive to my own struggles in the same arena. I recall his toil and the hours and love he gave to that endeavor. As he describes H. E. Phillip's tears when he gave up "The Paper," in effect he is describing his own that would come years later. Connie W. Adams was perhaps the most balanced editor of the past sixty years. In fact, of all words used to describe *Searching the Scriptures*, the term "balanced" is used more than any other.

Any biography or autobiography will reflect the unique perspective of the author. It cannot be otherwise. My father has sought to reveal his heart and his understanding of the times. You will find his story to be compelling, written with clarity, and deserving much consideration.

One more thing . . . "I am not worthy to walk in his shadow."

February 24, 2009
Murfreesboro, TN

Chapter 1

MY FIRST GOSPEL MEETING

It was a Saturday in June, 1950. I will never forget it. A small congregation which met on "the nine foot road" (that was the width of the pavement) a few miles out of Newport, North Carolina, had agreed for me to come and preach in my very first gospel meeting. The arrangements had been made months before through Harry Pickup, Sr. who had preached much in that community and had baptized a number of the members who comprised the congregation. Whether he had been asked to come and could not because of a schedule conflict or he just wanted to help a young preacher, I do not recall now. By that summer I had completed two years at Florida Christian College (now Florida College), had decided to stay out of school a year and preach for the church at Lake City, Florida, which work was to begin in July of that summer. In August I was to take unto myself a wife.

To say the least, the occasion was grandiose in the imagination of a young preacher who had not yet seen his twentieth birthday. My old rusty '41 Chevrolet was left in Virginia with my parents and my grand entrance into town was to be made on the bus. The local bus line to which I changed in Raleigh for the rest of the trip, stopped at nearly every crossroad. As the miles passed through corn, soy bean, cotton, and tobacco fields, the prospect of brethren waiting to greet me and thoughts of crowds of hearers filled my mind.

What problems might one expect in such an eight day meeting? Whatever they were, this young preacher was prepared for *everything*, at least I thought so at the time. I had one large suitcase with clothes neatly packed in it by my mother (I never could get them back in the same space they came out of). In addition, I had packed *every book I owned* in a medium sized metal footlocker.

Luckily, it had a handle on it, but also felt like it was full of bricks. The driver specifically asked if that was what I had in there when he unloaded it from the baggage compartment.

Now why did I take every book I had? Well, you never know what error you might confront in a strange community, or what hard question might be dropped in the question box (a common practice in meetings then). I had my Bible, *Johnson's Notes*, a Methodist *Discipline*, a Baptist *Manual*, an Episcopalian *Prayer Book*, the *Book of Mormon*, an Adventist *Manual*, a Lutheran *Catechism*, *Nichol's Pocket Bible Encyclopedia*, a large book for Family Bible Reading which my parents had earlier bought, unsuspectingly, from an Adventist door-to-door salesman, and an odd assortment of other books, most of which I had bought in connection with classes I had taken at Florida Christian College. Folks, I was ready! To complete my baggage, my "briefcase" was actually a bright green skate box. How, where, or why I had obtained that, I have no earthly idea. I have never owned a pair of skates in my life, can't stand up on them even now, and was reared a good distance from a paved road, and miles from the nearest sidewalk. But that skate box was my one and only briefcase for sometime. In it I carried my Bible, every sermon outline I had thus far obtained, plus class notes from college, some stationary, stamps, and other odds and ends. Yes, sir, I was ready! Or so I thought.

It was disconcerting when the bus rolled past the sign identifying Newport and then stopped right beside the highway. There was no bus station, not even a clearly marked bus stop, *and no brethren in sight to greet me*. The driver got off, unloaded my suitcase, footlocker, and green "briefcase," set them on the side of the road and drove off, leaving me to savor the fumes from the bus as it disappeared from sight, and to wonder, "Now what do I do?" Across the road was a barber shop with several men surveying the scene and wondering who the young stranger was. I gathered up my gear (and that was not easy) and what little dignity I could locate, struggled across the road, went into the barber shop, and asked if anyone in there was a member of the church of Christ, or knew of one in town. Finally, one man said he thought the couple who ran the general store back up the road about a hundred yards went "out there on the nine foot road."

With gear gathered up again, and with great difficulty, I made my way to the general store. There were several people sitting around and they all looked me over. I spotted a man behind the counter and said, "Are you a member of the church of Christ which meets out on the nine foot road?" He looked surprised for a moment and said, "I guess so, but my wife is better at going out there than I am." I said, "Well, I am the preacher for the meeting" and gave him my best smile. He just stared at me, called out to his wife and said, "Did you hear anything about them having a meetin' out there at church?" She walked over and said, "No, I was there Sunday, and don't remember hearing anything about it." This was not how this was supposed to turn out. Somehow, all the glamour of the grand arrival had disappeared. But then they thought of a relative who lived nearby who was very active in the church and called this good brother and wife to come down and check out this young fellow.

When these good people arrived, they had no recollection of any plans for a meeting. They loved brother Pickup and surmised that anyone he would recommend must be all right. But to be on the safe side, they quizzed me as to where I stood on the instrument, premillennialism, cups and classes, and several other things. Finally, I satisfied them and they invited me to go home with them until we could determine what course of action to take. They called a good brother, who took a leading part and later became one of the elders, to come and talk with me. Brother Pickup had converted him (and almost made him lose his crop because Pickup followed him up and down the row discussing the Bible with him). This brother lived several miles out in the country but between town and the meeting house. He came in a hurry. I liked him right away and have considered him a good friend ever since. But he wanted to be sure about me also, so I was interrogated again.

Then it suddenly dawned on him that "back about last February" brother Pickup had written to one of the brethren about having a young man come for a meeting. They met and discussed it, agreed to it, one of them sent me a letter giving a date in June, and then everyone forgot about it – that is, except for me. When they got all the pieces of the puzzle put together, they were terribly embarrassed, apologetic, but determined that, since I was there and so well recommended by such a beloved brother, we were going to have a meeting! And have one we did. The news spread quickly by word of mouth, from farm to farm, to the general stores in the county, and the meeting began right on schedule the next morning with the little frame building packed and children seated all around my feet on the platform. And so it continued for eight glorious days. I preached ten times on the following subjects: "God Has Spoken," "Rightly Dividing the Word," "The Gospel of Christ," "So Great Salvation," "Is Christ Divided," "The Church Jesus Built," "Instrumental Music In Worship," "Brazen Shields," "Does It Make a Difference?" and "What God Hath Joined

Together." The family which came to meet me at the store kept me in their home and showed much kindness.

With some exceptions, the meeting went well. I talked so much during my interrogations that I had about lost my voice by Sunday night and struggled all week with warm salt water and various home remedies which gave little relief. In addition, amid all my careful preparation, I neglected to bring a single necktie. I had a full suitcase, a full footlocker of books, a bright green "brief-case" full of notes, but not one single tie! Boy, was I ready! The good brother where I stayed offered me one of his ties. He was past middle age, had a lim-ited selection, and none which seemed to fit with a 19-year-old. But beggars can't be choosers, so I picked out one and wore it every time I preached. I also learned that a good assortment of ties would have been as helpful as the books I brought along. I was invited into homes for meals where people asked me Bible questions I had never even thought about, much less being prepared to give any kind of a sensible answer. And besides that, there was not a Mormon in one thousand miles of eastern North Carolina. I would gladly have traded my Book of Mormon for one youthful looking tie!

Well, that was the first of what has now grown to 840 gospel meetings. That first meeting opened the door for meetings in New Jersey, Ohio, and Tennes-see, because of brethren visiting there that week from those places. The echoes from the nine foot road have now been heard in forty states and fifteen coun-tries. On the advice of an older preacher I have kept a record of each meeting, the subjects preached, the number who responded to the gospel call, and what the brethren paid me for my efforts. That has been useful in figuring income taxes through the years.

The church on the nine foot road moved into the town of Newport into a nice brick building. My brother, Wiley, worked twice with them as local preach-er. In spite of my initial disillusionment, I will always be thankful to Harry Pickup, Sr. for opening that door for an unknown young preacher and also to the church on the nine foot road for giving me a hearing and encouraging me in the faith. They taught me much more than I taught them. There is often a wide gap between idealism and reality and no preacher can ever succeed until he learns to build a bridge across that gap.

Chapter 2

How It All Began

I was born on September 22, 1930 in a duplex on Tenth Street in Hopewell, Virginia, an industrial city located at the confluence of the James and Appomattox Rivers. My parents moved there from eastern North Carolina and for a while both of them worked in a silk mill. Joyner Wilson Adams was a strong man physically who had helped his father farm and work in timber. My mother, Nollie Stotesberry, had moved to Hopewell in 1923 when her mother came to run a boarding house, mostly for employees of the silk mill. In a few months my father followed. Joyner and Nollie were married on December 23, 1923 at the Christian Church. They were married between Sunday School and morning worship.

The Great Depression had begun in 1929. Like many others, my family was greatly affected by it. Times were hard. Jobs and money were scarce. The mid-1930's were the most difficult for us. As a child, I was not aware that we were poor. We were in the same situation as most of the people we knew. My father moved us to Chesterfield County in 1931 to what was called "the Vaughn farm." The big farm house accommodated our family and several relatives. There was plenty of food which we raised ourselves and shared with other people. When I was four years old, my father borrowed $500 and bought a five acre tract of land not far from the Appomattox River in the Rivermont community. It was all in woods. My father cleared a spot and built a small four room house out of rough lumber, which he cut from the clearing. The "walls" were thick, brown paper. With the help of an uncle, a thirty foot well was dug which supplied water for the house and livestock for years to come. In 1940, after a steady job was secured at Hercules, a loan was secured and the house was widened by ten feet and a second floor was added with four additional rooms, making a good sized farm house. There, Wiley and I grew up. In 1939 our sister, Glenda, arrived. By then, our grandmother had moved in to live with us.

The Adams home in Chesterfield County, Virginia

"Grandmammy," as we called her, was my mother's mother. What a treasure she was. She not only helped with the housework, canning, and cooking, but also in the garden and with other outside chores. She also taught me to fish and hunt. She was a dead shot with a rifle. From her I learned many lessons for life. She was fun-loving. Often at night, we would play checkers on a homemade checker board. She would set traps and taught me how to do that. When I fell into one of hers and would lose the game, she would chuckle and remind me to be careful and watchful. Then when the game was over, she would say, "Connie, get me the Book." She would read the Bible to me and, as I grew older, I would read it to her. After I began to show some interest in preaching, she said to me, "Son, if you are going to preach, don't be a jackleg preacher. Do it right." My parents set good examples before us and were consistent about attending church services, but I owe my "Grandmammy" a debt of gratitude for her influence in my life.

Until I was eleven years old, we attended the Christian Church in Hopewell. It began as a very conservative congregation. Over time, that changed. A preacher named Taylor was engaged. He was bent on getting the congregation connected with the Virginia Christian Missionary Society. He appointed what he called "The Preacher's Cabinet." While there were elders (who served only for one year), the "Cabinet" dominated the activities of the church. There were plays in the basement, Halloween parties, rummage sales, barbecue suppers, and entertainment. We had Christmas pageants. In the "junior department," I was one of the three wise men. When I was eight years old, I made my debut as an entertainer on a Mother's Day program. I had learned three chords on the guitar (with the reluctant tutoring of my brother, Wiley), and sang "If I Could Hear My Mother Pray Again." While I was on the program in the basement, Wiley was upstairs performing with his guitar and a girl who played an accordion. Wiley was a member of the Christian Church and was active in "Christian Endeavor," a youth organization. Along with these social activities, there was also a change in direction in the preaching. The old, basic first principle sermons were gone.

When I was ten, there was an annual church meeting during which it was proposed that the local preacher should exchange pulpits with the various denominational preachers in town. My father opposed it and said something to the effect that, if they were wrong in what they taught, we should have no part in it, and, if they were right, we ought to close up and join them. Others made similar objections. One of the "Cabinet" members arose and said, "The trouble with brother Adams and these other objectors is that they are trying to live in the days of the horse and buggy. This is the day of the automobile and, if the church does not keep up with the times, it will be left behind." I never forgot that. I have lived to see the same attitude manifested by brethren who have grown weary with "the old paths" and who, like the Athenians, want to hear "some new thing."

This dissatisfaction came to a head when I was eleven years old. Ed Craddock, from Nashville, Tennessee, came to hold a gospel meeting with the small congregation which met in a store front building in Colonial Heights. Some family friends from North Carolina, who had left the Christian Church and were now members of the church, convinced our parents that they ought to go hear this man "just preach the Bible." So, we all loaded up in the old 1936 Chevrolet and went. That was back before seat belts and car seats for children. You just piled as many in the car as you could and still close the door! It did not matter if you had to sit on someone's lap. The meeting was different from what we had been seeing at the Christian Church. There was no instrument. A man got up, announced a song number, and just started singing and all joined in. The first song I heard without an instrument was "Oh To Be Like Thee." Craddock preached on "The New Testament Church."

On our way home things were quiet until my father asked, "Well, what did you think of that?" Our Grandmammy spoke up quickly and said, "I'll tell you one thing; it was every word according to the Bible. He quoted one hundred and ten verses, for I wrote them down." We returned every night the rest of that meeting and a number of our friends from the Christian church in Hopewell did as well. After that two week meeting, and with the interest shown from Hopewell, it was decided to rent a store front in Hopewell and have Ed Craddock come and preach for two weeks there. By the end of that meeting, my parents and over thirty others made their decision. They left the Christian church, renouncing its errors, and formed a church of Christ in Hopewell. The new congrega-

Joyner W. and Nollie Adams celebrate thier 50th Wedding Anniversary.

tion continued to meet in the storefront on Broadway until a union hall was purchased on Cawson Street. I was baptized at the age of twelve in a creek in Chesterfield County. Leaving the Christian Church was not easy. We had many friends and relatives who remained in that denomination. Family and friendship ties were strained. During the days leading up to this decision, the subject was discussed at the family supper table. Respect for Bible authority was impressed on me at a young age. But through it all, I learned that you can stand on principle without becoming bitter. We never saw any rancor. There was sadness at having to sever cherished ties. In later years when there were problems in the church and a stand had to be taken, that same spirit was shown by my parents.

A Visiting Preacher

When I was twelve, we kept a visiting preacher in our home during a ten day gospel meeting. My mother was uneasy about it because we did not have a bathroom in the house and we lacked other amenities. My father did not understand what the problem was, since we lived that way all the time. They painted the room where he was to stay and our mother borrowed some extra dishes from her sisters. Bonds Stocks was the preacher who came down from Washington, D.C. He had gone to Washington to work as a secretary for Senator J. C. Rankin from Mississippi. Brother Stocks had met many important people, including Franklin D. Roosevelt. But he was called on to do some preaching and was so able in that work that brethren prevailed on him to leave his government job and devote his life entirely to preaching. I was fascinated with this guest in our home. He had many humorous things to tell, and we were all rapt listeners to his stories of experiences in what seemed like far away places. We learned that he was brought up about as poor as we were. For some reason, he nicknamed me "Cornelius."

One day he invited me to ride over to town with him to service his car. On the way, he asked, "Cornelius, what are you going to do when you grow up?" I said, "My brother Wiley and I are going to Nashville, Tennessee and play on the Grand Ole Opry." Wiley was five years older, and already had organized a band. We played on radio station WSSV in Petersburg, Virginia three nights a week sponsored by a clothing store. We also played in school auditoriums, usually sponsored by the PTA, a garden club, or the police department. In my youthful naiveté, I figured that, with our background and experience, they would want to put us right on stage as soon as they found out we were in town. If he was surprised by my answer, he didn't show it. He said, "Well, that sounds like fun, but did you ever think of being a gospel preacher?" I said, "No Sir, I don't think I could do that. I wouldn't know what to say." He thought a minute and then asked, "Does it make you nervous to sing and play in front of an audience?" "No," I said, "I kinda like it." He said, "See there, you already have stage fright licked."

Nothing more was said until we started back home. He said, "You know, I have some notes I have typed up about church history. I have put a lot of work into that. While I am here, you could copy those, if you wanted to. You never know when you might need some of that information." As soon as we got home, I rushed in and found some paper and a pen and sat down at the kitchen table to begin copying those notes. It took several sessions to complete the job. At the time, I did not realize that his unexpected question had turned my life around. He planted a seed in my heart and I have never been able to get rid of it. I have thought of that experience many times when I have stayed in the home of brethren who had children about the age I was when Bonds Stocks came to stay with us. I have said to a number of little boys, "I hope I get to hear you preach sometime." You never know where that may lead.

The Influence of a Local Preacher

In my early teens Arley E. Moore, a Texan, came to preach at Cawson Street. He took much interest in training the young people. He started a training class and had boys, including me, reading Scripture, leading prayer, making talks, and leading singing. When I was fourteen, in August, 1945, we visited my paternal grandfather at Pike Road, North Carolina. The church there did not have a full time preacher. I was asked to lead the singing on Sunday morning and at the end of the service, I made a short talk and extended the invitation. That seemed to surprise some. Arthur Respass, who took a leading part in the work, arose and said there would be a service that night with preaching and they should all come to see who would preach. Not one word was said to me directly that I would be the preacher. But my father told me that I should collect my thoughts just in case. That night, about five minutes before time for meeting to begin, brother Respass walked over to me and said, "Young man, I think the folks are expecting to hear something from you." With the help of Arley Moore, I had prepared an outline some weeks before and so, when the time came, I arose and spoke for twenty minutes on "The Excuses of Moses." That was my first attempt at preaching a sermon. After we returned to Virginia, word spread and I was called on to speak by appointment at Colonial Heights and at two places in Richmond, as well as at Cawson Street.

When I was seventeen, the elders at Cawson Street decided to have a tent meeting in Davisville, a largely Black area of Hopewell. They sent to St. Petersburg, Florida for John R. Vaughner, a very able preacher, who had studied under the famed Marshall Keeble. Brother Vaughner brought with him another preacher, Raymond Dunwood, to lead singing and to be his "reader" as the custom was. When the tent meeting began, there were no Black Christians in Hopewell. When it was over, three weeks later, there were 147! Arrangements were made for Raymond Dunwood to come and work with them, but he had committed to working with brother Vaughner in meetings for the next six months. They needed someone to preach until he returned. The elders (my father was one of them) asked me if I would preach for them during that time if the brethren agreed. I said, "Yes." With the financial help of John W. Akin of Dallas, Texas and the labor of my father and others, a building was erected on the lot where the tent had been pitched. We met under that tent for several weeks. The experience was rich for me. Most of the members had been converted from the Baptist church (including the preacher and his wife and every deacon except one). They were not hesitant to "amen" the preaching, and made me feel like I was preaching, whether I was or not.

One Sunday night I was preaching on the need to go beyond first principles and live godly lives. I observed that, if you were a gambler, a drinker, used bad language, or were fooling around with someone else's wife, repentance demanded you quit such sins. At that point, an older brother stood up, turned around and pointed to a young man seated behind him and in a loud, clear voice said, "That's you he's talkin' about." I was stunned, and the young man was petrified and looked as if he wanted to crawl under the seat. But they say a sermon without application is not worth much! One thing is certain; they taught me a lot more than I taught them.

During that tent meeting, we were able to witness a scene that is deeply implanted in my memory. Of those 147 who were baptized, eighty-seven of them were baptized one Sunday afternoon in a lake. That was the most I ever saw baptized on a single occasion. In the Philippines, in 1999, we saw forty-three baptized on one occasion, and thirty-seven on another.

Arley Moore influenced me in another way. When I was sixteen, he hired me that summer to work in his office preparing a card file on articles in the *Firm Foundation* and the *Gospel Advocate*. He had issues of those periodicals from the 1920's. That experience introduced me to the names and writings of many good men. It also generated in me an interest in religious papers and helped me to realize the value of such writing, even long after the authors were dead. Little did I know then what a part religious journals would have in my own life and work. Arley Moore influenced me in another way which was to become a part of my life. He and his family had spent some time in Seward, Alaska before Alaska had gained statehood. He showed us many pictures about his work there, including one of him baptizing a man in icy water. Somehow that image stayed with me. It also stirred within me a desire to preach in far away places.

Arley and Happy Moore

By the time high school days were over and I headed to Florida to get a college education, there was already a fire burning in my heart to spend my life preaching the gospel. I was not going to Florida Christian College to become a preacher. I was already preaching at every opportunity. My parents and I agreed that some college training would prepare me to do my work better, and I needed all the help I could get.

Chapter 3

School on the Banks of the Hillsborough River

Late one night in early September, 1948, Martin Lemon and I boarded the Silver Meteor, a train which ran from New York City to Tampa, Florida, then on to Miami. We were headed for Florida Christian College, located in Temple Terrace on the banks of the Hillsborough River. My parents wanted me to go to college and made great personal sacrifices to help me all they could. My father wore the same suit on Sundays for a long time and my mother wore the same dress on Sundays as well. They raised chickens and truck farmed in addition to Daddy's job at Hercules. At the time, I did not fully realize how much they sacrificed for me. My mother wept much at the thought of my leaving home. She would seclude herself in the bedroom for long periods of time and try to compose herself before coming back into our presence, but her red eyes told the story.

My brother, Wiley, was not altogether pleased with my decision to go away to college. He was married and worked as a chemist in the lab at Hercules. But he also had formed a band called the "The Dixie Boys" which played on the radio and performed in school auditoriums. I was one of the Dixie Boys. So was Martin Lemon. Martin was our fiddler and comedian. He had finished high school a couple of years before and was working as a meat cutter for the Safeway Food Store in Hopewell. He was reared in the mountains of Virginia, west of Roanoke. When he began playing music with us, we persuaded him to go to church services with us. He became very interested and obeyed the gospel. He became interested in preaching and decided to go to Florida with me. That meant that Wiley had to find another guitar man and fiddler. Even after I had been at Florida Christian College a few weeks, Wiley wrote me and said he respected my desire to preach the gospel, but when I realized that I could not make a success of that noble work, I could still come back home and take my place with the Dixie Boys.

Truth be told, I was not good college material. I had not been a good student in high school. I failed algebra and geometry and had to repeat them to graduate. I did well in English, grammar, literature, and history. But

Wiley (age 15) and Connie (age 10) – The original Dixie boys.

math and science baffled me. I did well in Latin and that has proved to be a great help to me in my later studies. I had a great time in high school, but am ashamed of my poor grades. After our mother died in 1995, I found, among her many keepsakes, my school report cards. I had forgotten just how bad they were and decided to destroy them lest some grandchild should ever discover them and use them as an excuse not to do his best. With the present standards at Florida College, I would have been admitted on academic probation, if at all. All through high school years, I had taken great interest in the Bible and things related to that. I worked hard on preparations for sermons and read the *Gospel Advocate* which came every week. I was especially fascinated with the "News and Notes" section. The writers became heroes in my mind and I counted it a special honor to actually meet some of them when they came into our area for meetings.

Martin Lemon and Connie performing at Florida Christian College

My grades at Florida Christian College were not all that great. It took awhile to learn how to really study. The Bible classes were of the most interest to me. Some of the teachers had a profound influence on my life. L. R. Wilson was the president at that time. My father had driven me to Arlington, Virginia to meet him when I was a senior in high school. After hearing him speak and talking with him privately, I decided that is where I needed to go. James R. Cope became president at the beginning of my sophomore year. At thirty-two, he was the youngest college president in the country. He was a handsome man and his wife, Georgia Dean, was a stunningly beautiful woman. I think the college girls envied her and the boys envied him. Classes under L. R. Wilson, James R. Cope, Bill Humble, Clinton Hamilton, and Pat Hardeman were rich. Homer Hailey was there my last two years and his classes were rewarding and challenging. To this day, I have, and use, class notes made during those four years.

The college initially had a high school with boarding students. It began as a four year college. After James R. Cope became president, the board decided to convert it to a junior college. Those who had enrolled under the four year program were allowed to graduate. I was in the last class to receive a four year degree, graduating in the spring of 1953. In that small class were Melvin Curry, John Clark, and Cecil Willis

James R. Cope

When Martin Lemon and I arrived in Tampa, we were met by Arley Moore who had moved to St. Petersburg by then. We were in a world different from anything we had ever seen. As we left Sulphur Springs, we drove on a narrow, two-lane road, known then as the Temple Terrace Highway (now Busch Boulevard). It looked desolate with several miles of palmetto brush as far as we could see. When we finally reached Temple Terrace, there was one two story building on the right which had a gas station. That was it. Then we began to see houses with Spanish type architecture. Some of them were quite elegant. Streets wound around a golf course. The main campus stretched along a curved street across from the golf course and was situated on the banks of the picturesque Hillsborough River. Cypress trees with Spanish moss hanging from the branches lined the banks of the river.

The college facilities were limited, to say the least. We were placed in South Cottage in a fairly large room shared by four of us, Martin Lemon, Earl Kimbrough, Charles Kilgore, and me. We made a solemn pact that should anyone of us become interested in a certain girl, the rest of us would back off, and we all honored that pact. None of the rooms was air conditioned, but most of the students had not enjoyed that luxury at home. Some thought the rules for student conduct were too strict, but they were no more so than what I had been used to at home in Virginia. We lived in the South Cottage with veterans from World War II. These young men were older than some of the rest of us and I am convinced that the administration allowed them a little more leeway than those in the other dorms. We were allowed to leave the campus on dates on Friday nights, provided we double dated. Not many students had cars and those who did were glad to share them with the rest. One night, Martin Lemon and I had a hoedown going past lights out time. What became North Cottage was, at that time, where L. R. Wilson and family lived, the president's home. It was only a few feet from South Cottage. About fifteen minutes into our hoedown, there was a loud knock on the door. There stood Leonard Lewis, the dean of students (and of the college), in his bathrobe and with his hair uncombed, an incongruous sight, for he was normally a somber man. Sister Wilson had called him and asked if he would quiet down "those Virginia hillbillies," so she and the children could get some sleep. I am still of the opinion that he was more upset with her for awakening him than he was with us.

That year there were not more than 150 students. Half of them were young men, and probably 75% of them planned to preach the gospel. Young men were so eager to preach that they were willing to hitchhike to meet speaking appointments. There was a Sowers Club for those interested in preaching. We had a few visiting speakers but most of the time we practiced making short talks which were critiqued by a Bible faculty member. While that was painful at times, it was most helpful. If anyone was offended by the constructive criticism, he kept it to himself. We had sham debates.

During my freshman year, I was invited to preach on Sundays at Cortez, a fishing village on the Gulf of Mexico, about forty-five miles south of Tampa. I did not have a car then and a fellow student from Virginia, an ex-G.I., agreed to drive me down each week if I would pay for the gas. They paid me $15 a week and I gave Bill Echols $5 for gas. That summer I worked with the church at Lake Wales and lived in a large boarding house. The church was small, but we had a good summer and baptized several people. It was a lonely summer since there were not many young people my age in the church, so I was glad when school started. I continued to preach there during my second school year. They paid me $25 a week. Just before going to Lake Wales for the summer, I bought a car, a 1936 Graham Page. It cost $295 and I paid the balance due that summer.

Lake Wales church building.

I drove it home at the Christmas break, to Virginia. By then it was using a lot of oil. Before the trip, I bought a two gallon can of oil on sale from the gas station near the school and thought surely that eight quarts of oil would get Martin Lemon and me home. But we poured the last drop of that oil into the crank case at Yulee, Florida, 200 miles from Tampa, with 650 more miles to go!

Martin Lemon kept count and it took 26 quarts of oil to get us home. All that pollution might have been the start of global warming! My uncle Howard, a very good mechanic, put new piston rings in it while we were home.

Near the beginning of my second year, I had met a cute little freshman from Fulton, Kentucky, named Barbara Rose Colley. I was smitten and so was she. We had planned for Martin to ride back to Tampa with someone else and I was going to drive that Graham (with the new rings) from Hopewell, Virginia to Fulton, Kentucky (a 900 mile trip). Then, we were to join up with George LeMasters and his girl friend, who was also from western Kentucky, to drive straight through to Tampa and back to school. I mapped out the route (there were no interstates then), but I failed to count up the distance or to figure how long it would take. I left home in Virginia at midnight on New Year's Day in a thirteen-year-old car with no heater and no radio. Because of the new piston rings, I could not drive over forty-five miles an hour for the first 200 miles. It was cold weather all the way. I wore a heavy car coat, toboggan, and gloves and part of the time kept a blanket over my lap. My mother had packed plenty of food. Early morning found me in the mountains of eastern Kentucky. I stopped to buy gas and asked the attendant (who looked me over rather suspiciously), "How far is it to Fulton? I'm supposed to be there for supper tonight?" He said, "Whur?" I said, "Fulton." He said, "I never heered of it." I showed him Fulton on the map and he said, "Young feller, I'd be surprised if you get there for supper tomorrow night." Well, it was not quite that bad, but it did take me until midnight (Fulton is on central time), exactly twenty-five hours. But don't laugh, I was in love! And I'd do it all again. I sang until I was hoarse, whistled, quoted every verse of Scripture I could remember, and prayed a lot. The next morning my battery was dead. My future father-in-law, with his pickup truck, had to push to get started and went with me to get the battery charged. Or so I thought. I learned later that he had told the man, "Put a new battery in that thing and send me the bill. My daughter has to ride to Tampa in that car."

Bobbie and I became serious about planning a life together. We spent much time sitting on the bank of the river and dreaming of our life and work together. She had preachers in her family. A. O. Colley and his sons, Flavil Colley and R. L. Colley, were well known in west Tennessee, western Kentucky, and Texas. We dreamed about spending some of our life in a foreign land sowing the seed of the kingdom. We decided to get married in Fulton on August 14, 1950, two days before her nineteenth birthday, and a little more than a month before my twentieth. When she wrote to her parents and told them of our plans, her mother rode a bus to Tampa for the express purpose of talking us out of it. She alternated between trying to persuade Bobbie and me. She talked to both of us (one at a time) up and down that river. We were too young. Bobbie needed to finish her education. Even as late as May when school was out and they came down to drive Bobbie back home to Fulton, she would not let up. Finally, Bobbie's father, Doron Colley, had heard enough. He said, "Virginia, you might as well hush. They are going to get married." And he was right.

Just before school was out that spring, James R. Cope called me into his office and asked about our plans. He knew my parents were having a hard time financially helping me at school and that I owed quite a balance which I hoped to settle during the summer. He told me he would not promise anything, but that he knew a brother who liked to help promising young preachers but that, if he helped, he did not want his name to ever be used. My second gospel meeting that summer was at Baker, Florida in the panhandle of the state. Bobbie was at Fulton planning the wedding. She wrote me every day of that ten day meeting. One day I received a letter from brother Cope telling me that the brother he had mentioned to me, had settled what I owed on my school bill. To this day, I do not know who this benefactor was, but I shall ever be thankful for this kindness.

Connie and Barbara (Bobbie) (1950).

First Located Work and Marriage

After the meeting at Newport, North Carolina, I moved to Lake City, Florida to my first located work. We had decided to stay out of school for a year and then, if possible, to go back for two more years. I found an upstairs, partially furnished, apartment on Franklin Street in Lake City. The church was to pay us $45 a week out of which we paid $45 a month for rent, and had a car payment of $45 a month. That left $90 for food, clothing, gasoline, and to somehow furnish the apartment with what we needed to live.

The wedding was beautiful. It was

Lake City, Florida church building (1950).

held at Bobbie's uncle's house. It had a long, winding staircase and we stood in front of a huge fireplace and mantle and pledged our love to each other "till death do us part." By then I had traded the Graham for a 1941 Chevrolet. It had seen better days. Everyone assumed we would be driving that on our honeymoon to the Smoky Mountains. I had hung some clothes in the back, as a decoy. Mr. Colley had offered to let us drive his almost new Mercury on the honeymoon. We had all our things for the trip in the trunk and the car was parked across the street headed the opposite direction from my car and others whose owners planned to follow us out of town. My brother, Wiley, was the chief engineer in decorating my car. When we left and took off in that Mercury, their expressions were priceless. Some tried to give chase but the Mercury was too much for them. They decided they still ought to have some fun out of it. The Colleys were to drive our car while we were gone. So with "just married" written across the back and with shoes and tin cans tied to the bumper, the procession followed them down Lake Street (Fulton's main street), blowing their horns and creating quite a commotion. But the Colleys were good sports about it all.

The church at Lake City numbered 90-100. They met in an old building with a bell tower and that needed much repair. The roof leaked when it rained. The baptistry was under the pulpit floor and sagged a little when I stood there to preach. They had had some trouble due to some views about the kingdom held by the former preacher. Some agreed with him and others did not. I was young and inexperienced and had my work cut out for me. Early on, Bobbie proved to be wise beyond her years. She was a good money manager, such as we had to manage. She also handled the issue of living in the fishbowl with ease. She was not easily rattled, took things in stride, and was not too sensitive to criticism. We had not been there long before one of the sisters came over one day to fill her in on all the gossip about some with whom she had a difference. Bobbie said, "Wait, let me write all this down and take it with us. When Connie gets home, he will want you to go with us to see these folks so we can work all this out." Well, the lady nearly passed out, said she would not think of doing such a thing, and that she ought to be going. That ended that. I marvel to this day at the wisdom of that nineteen-year-old preacher's wife.

First Encounter with a Sponsoring Church

Billy Hood was the preacher at Nebraska Avenue in Tampa and he started a radio program which was carried on several stations in Florida. The church at Lake City became involved in it. They sent money to the church at Nebraska Avenue to pay for the Sunday morning program and Nebraska Avenue in turn sent a recording to the radio station in Lake City which was only two blocks from our building. It did not seem right to me and I made a trip to Tampa to talk with Billy Hood about it. He was rather dismissive about it but assured me that what they were doing was all right. I went out to the college and talked with Bill Humble about it. I remembered a class he taught on Restoration History in which we had studied the missionary society and also the practice of the sponsoring church in which a congregation assumed a work greater than it could finance and solicited funds from other churches to provide the service. In the class, Bill Humble said the sponsoring church was a missionary society under an eldership and that it violated the principle of 1 Peter 5:2 which said elders should "tend the flock of God among you." Brother Humble said what Nebraska Avenue was doing was wrong for that reason. When I returned to Lake City, I attempted to study the matter with the brethren but they dismissed it all as much ado about nothing and left me to understand that I was young and inexperienced and did not need to be a hobby rider. But I did not forget all of that when the Herald of Truth radio program began, sponsored by the Fifth and Highland church in Abilene, Texas in 1951.

Back to School

Our year at Lake City convinced me that I needed to go back to school. I was again invited to preach at Cortez during the school year. Bobbie also went to school to complete her A.A while I worked toward my B.A. Her parents paid her tuition, but not mine. We had very meager resources. We rented a small

Slim (Connie), Cedric (Weldon Warnock), and Cousin Clarence (Wiley). This picture appeared on the cover of *SPOTLIGHT*, an entertainerment magazine for the west coast of Florida.

garage apartment from a nice family in Temple Terrace. They had citrus trees and told us to help ourselves. Between grapefruit, oranges, Spam, and Dinty Moore canned beef stew, we managed to survive. The folks at Cortez sensed that things were tough for us and would often send us home with fresh fish. I still don't like Spam.

At the beginning of my third year, Wiley and his family had arrived at Florida Christian College. He had begun preaching after I left home for college and had developed that fire in his bones which would not go out. They had two children. My mother kept them so Wilma, Wiley's wife, could work and they could pay off all their debts before beginning their college adventure. We soon got acquainted with Weldon Warnock who had come from eastern Kentucky. He played a fiddle and a guitar and became a fast friend. Since times were so tough financially for all of us, I proposed to Wiley and Weldon that we revive the Dixie Boys and see if we could earn some money to keep bread on the table. We started with a Saturday afternoon show on WHBO in Sulphur Springs,

TAMPA SUNDAY TRIBUNE, Sunday, May 16, 1954   13-C

WFLA HOEDOWN STARS—The Dixie Boys, one of the funniest hillbilly groups in the South, keep the audience rocking with their antics at the Saturday night WFLA Hoedown at the Municipal Auditorium. Left to right, they are Pa, Slim, Cedric and Clarence.

Phota taken during a live performance at Municipal Auditorium. It appeared in the *Tampa Tribune*.

"the little station with a lot of listeners." We called on several businesses who agreed to pay for advertising on our program. This paid for the radio time and provided us with a little extra. We advertised for Copeland's Market (Lloyd Copeland was one of the board members of the college), for Williams Brothers Used Cars, for Brecheens Barbeque, and a few others. This show generated invitations for shows in schools and other public auditoriums. After a few months, a Saturday night three hour country music show was started at the Municipal Auditorium, a venue which seated 2,300 people and hosted various performers, including some from the Grand Ole Opry in Nashville, Tennessee. We auditioned for the show and were hired on the spot. We formed a comedy act in which we did parodies of popular songs, played off key on purpose, told jokes, and generally kept the audience in an uproar. We were known as Slim (that was me), Cedric (Weldon), and Cousin Clarence (Wiley).

While we appeared at various times during the three hour show, we were featured on the 9-9:30 show sponsored by Royal Crown Cola. We even sang the commercial jingle with which that show started and ended. That portion was carried on WFLA radio. This show became a popular tourist attraction as well as having local interest. We hired a bass fiddle player whom we called "Pa." Offers came to perform in a number of places throughout central and the west coast of Florida. We usually did these shows on Friday nights and put together a two hour performance with a mixture of country, blue grass, and comedy. This did help us to survive.

But the Devil never quits. Country music has always had songs about cheating and drinking. We resolved early on to choose what songs we could perform and which ones we could not. We never played in a place where there was drinking or dancing. We had job offers from clubs but always turned them down. If there was anything off-color it usually was in comedy. Since we *were* the comedy act on the WFLA HOEDOWN, we had control of that. As our act became better known, we were called on to perform "warm-up" or "opening" sets for some of the Grand Ole Opry performers who came for concerts at the same venue where we played every Saturday night. We "opened" for Marty Robbins, Ray Price, Kitty Wells, and others. Most of them were very kind to us. But there were also temptations aplenty. We met some performers who were wayward Christians. It is hard to succeed in that business and keep your head on straight. One Saturday night, we were "scouted" by an agent from New Orleans who worked with a well known booking agency. They booked acts from Nashville, Dallas, and Shreveport. Of course they got their fee but they also had managed some acts which gained much notoriety and wealth. We did not know he was there until after the show when he came backstage to the dressing room. He offered us an attractive proposal. We told him that we were gospel preachers and that we were playing music to help us finish school so we could get on with our lives in preaching. He shook his head but left his card and told us to call him if we changed our minds. I had wanted to preach since I was in my early teens. But I also loved performing. If there was such a thing as a "ham," then I was pure pork! I began to rationalize. Maybe we could travel and perform through the week, but fill preaching appointments on Sundays. Yes, that would work. Even if I convinced myself that was the thing to do, would I be able to convince Wiley and Weldon? Thankfully, they were content to stay with the original plan and that was to use this as a means to an end, with the end being far nobler than the means. But it troubled me so much that I went to Homer Hailey to seek advice. He was very kind and understanding. In fact, he

Homer Hailey (1952)

had been to our show a few times dressed in his western attire. He asked some questions which helped to put things in perspective. Gratitude for his wise counsel made it very difficult for me, years later, to take public issue with brother Hailey over his views on marriage, divorce, and remarriage. Through the years I have seen several good people who lost their way while trying to juggle an entertainment, sports, or political career with serving the Lord. Some things just don't mix. I still play now and then "for my own amazement." Yes, I still carry a guitar pick in my wallet. No self-respecting picker should ever get caught without a pick!

Chapter 4

Confronting Divisive Issues

The first issue of the *Gospel Guardian* I ever saw had an article on the front page by Cled Wallace entitled "That Rock Fight in Italy" (Vol. 1, Number 36, Jan. 19, 1950). The library at Florida Christian College had a shelf with recent issues of periodicals, such as the *Gospel Advocate, Firm Foundation, Vindicator, Gospel Broadcast, Gospel Guardian,* and others. Some of the brethren in Italy had been stoned by a mob led by angry priests when they were found baptizing in a lake near the pope's summer home. The wire services carried the story and so did *Life Magazine.* Church members had been encouraged to write their congressmen about it. The more of Cled Wallace's article I read, the more indignant I became. It was written with satirical wit and chided the brethren in Italy for being brash and untactful. He also questioned the sponsoring church concept by which the preachers in Italy were being supported. At first, all I could see was that our brethren were being persecuted for preaching the gospel. But I read other articles and found that they made sense. From then on, I would go to the library and seek out the latest issue of the paper. It did not take long to realize that there was a major conflict brewing.

After World War II, zealous and well-meaning brethren had promoted sponsoring church arrangements to spread the gospel in Italy, Germany, and Japan. The Union Avenue church in Memphis, Tennessee decided to sponsor the work in Japan, Broadway church in Lubbock, Texas took on the work in Germany, and the church in Brownfield, Texas the work in Italy. The plan was for the elders of these large churches to oversee the work in these places but for other congregations to send their funds to the sponsoring church elders to administer them. It became popular for any preacher going to work either in another country, or in a needy area of this country, to first locate a sponsoring church. The elders of these churches became "ecumenical elders" as I heard Foy E. Wallace, Jr. call them in 1955 when he worked with us in a meeting at Glenwood Hills in Decatur, Georgia.

In 1951 the Fifth and Highland church in Abilene, Texas became the sponsor for a national radio program (which later expanded to television). The plan was first conceived and practiced in Iowa by two young preachers, James D. Willeford and James Walter Nichols. They brought it to Abilene, first to the College church, which declined their proposal. But then Fifth and Highland agreed to oversee it. One of their elders, W. F. Cawyer, traveled the country soliciting support from congregations for this project. At first, the elders at Fifth and Highland said they were able to provide $1 for every $200 supplied by other churches. The excitement and euphoria generated by this much publicized work, gave way to controversy over the scripturality of the sponsoring church arrangement. Articles appeared in the *Gospel Advocate* and *Firm Foundation* supporting the plan, while articles in the *Gospel Guardian* opposed it. James Walter Nichols came to Florida College and was invited to speak on behalf of the Herald of Truth, as the program was named. That gave rise to discussions in Bible classes. Some thought it was a great thing, but others wondered if it was according to what is written.

The college lecture program became a battleground for several years in the 1950's. Otis Gatewood spoke one year about the work in Germany. He was touring the states and raising money for a large building in Frankfort, Germany. Questions arose after his speech and things got pretty heated. James D. Bales from Harding College came and defended the sponsoring church. Such men as Yater Tant, James W. Adams, J. Ed Nowlin, and others spoke in opposition. Every afternoon during these lecture weeks, there was an open forum. Franklin T. Puckett moderated these sometimes explosive sessions. Lines had not yet been drawn and brethren on both sides of the issue attended and had their say in these open forums. Franklin T. Puckett conducted these sessions with dignity and firmness.

In those days, the college at Temple Terrace was not afraid to take a stand. When it became obvious that the administration and faculty opposed not only the sponsoring church but also church support of benevolent homes, as well as church support of the colleges, an all out effort was launched to shut the school down. One wealthy board member threatened to withdraw his financial support if they did not fire James R. Cope. Other board members, led by Lee

Warren Boswell, made it clear that, while they would miss his help, they would manage.

The school was attacked in the influential *Gospel Advocate* on several occasions. The pool of prospective students began to shrink. Harry Pickup, Sr., who was public relations director, had to make student recruiting trips into the northeast to persuade students, some of whom were not Christians, to come to school in Florida. With great personal sacrifices from the board, administrators, and faculty, the school survived. Enemies of the school called it "that little anti college in Florida" and often tried to link the school with the *Gospel Guardian*, even referring to some of the faculty as "Guardian Boys."

Bible teachers at the school were militant. They imparted that spirit to some of the students. I say "some" because there were students who joined the institutional bandwagon. In classes where questions were studied that were controversial, teachers would fairly present varying views, but would not fail to take a stand for what that teacher thought was right. There was no "jump ball" teaching where something was left up in the air. The teaching was aimed at building faith and not creating doubt. In those years, I never heard anyone ask, "Is that a salvation issue?"

Student conduct was expected to meet a high standard. Girls were not allowed to wear pants to class and boys did not wear jeans. Students were not allowed to hold hands on campus. There was a time set for lights to be out. No student or faculty member was seen in shorts.

Were there students who broke the rules? Of course. Some were sent home. But a serious effort was made to provide a respectful atmosphere in which to study and grow. We had fun and plenty of it. The college has always mirrored the convictions and mores of the homes out of which the students have come. It has never been possible to please every constituent. One student got in a fight with another over a girl they both liked. One of them drew a knife. The discipline committee was about to send him home. He was a good hearted boy, generally, but was a little slow in many ways. During the week the discipline committee was dealing with this issue, this young man came forward at the midweek service of the church in Temple Terrace to confess his wrong which was certainly publicly known. Clinton Hamilton had offered an invitation at the end of the church service, and this young man responded. After a lengthy talk between the two of then, this boy arose and said, "Brother Hamilton asked me if I wanted him to make a statement for me and I told him I wanted to make my own statement. You know, the Bible says, 'Every tub shall sit on its own bottom', and it's time for me to sit on mine." They gave him another chance and so far as I know, there were no more such incidents.

Through the years, the college has had its share of critics. I have been one of them and that has included criticisms during every administration. But I have also been a friend to the college. With the deteriorating standards in public education, schools like Florida College have provided a wholesome atmosphere for young people just out of high school and has offered a bridge between leaving home and either higher education or the job market. Some have criticized it for being "a preacher factory" and have thought that it supplanted the church. If it is a "preacher factory," then it is not a very successful one, for very few of the students become gospel preachers. I was already doing my best to preach the gospel before enrolling there and that was true of most of the young men with whom I went to school who planned to spend their lives preaching. Only a few voices questioned their right to have a lecture program and those who did were generally influenced by the views of Daniel Sommer. Over the years, I have spoken on the annual lectures at least a dozen times. I don't recall having a meeting cancelled or my soundness called in question because of such participation. For several years I served on the National Council, an advisory group to the administration. After my first wife died, president Bob F. Owen wrote me a very kind letter inviting me to join the Bible faculty and outlining the classes I would teach. For several reasons, I decided not to accept that gracious offer. For a few years I served as president of the Kentuckiana Booster club to promote the interest of the college in Louisville and southern Indiana. We sold many truck loads of citrus and sponsored other projects to provide scholarships for students from that area. How many country music shows we have done to raise funds for various projects, I do not now recall. All of this has been stated to show that, if I have been a critic, it was out of love and concern for something near to my heart and from which I have received great benefit. Human institutions are just that, human institutions. Historically, such ventures tend to drift away from the original principles which gave them birth. Such dismal history does not mean that these projects were wrong in and of themselves. Let's face it. Churches which served a generation or two have gone astray. Where is the church in Jerusalem, Antioch, or Ephesus?

When schools or papers are started with noble intentions, they deserve to be praised for what good they do. When they leave the ground on which they once stood and begin to advocate and practice what is wrong, then they are fair game for criticism. The nature and extent of the criticism must be determined by the seriousness of the drifting which occurs. One of the dangers to be faced when schools leave their moorings is the loyalty of their alumni. Some do not become nearly as excited about criticizing departures in the church as they do when their alma mater is under scrutiny.

An Emotional Issue

In tandem with the sponsoring church question, was the church support of benevolent homes, especially orphan homes. While there were institutions for widows and for unwed mothers, by far, the greatest controversy was raised over churches supporting orphan homes from their treasuries. This issue was so emotionally charged that many were blinded by what they perceived to be an injustice to "poor little orphans." Nobody was opposed to caring for needy children. If the proponents of these institutions had managed them simply as private enterprises financed by good business practices and donations from interested individuals, there never would have been the division which did occur. Even the friends of these church supported institutions did not agree as to how they should be managed. For the most part, those west of the Mississippi River thought they should be operated under the oversight of elders of a church. Advocates east of that river thought they should be under boards of directors. The *Firm Foudation* opted for the former view while the *Gospel Advocate* took the latter view. So closely linked were the sponsoring church question and the church support of orphan homes that, when brethren began to have public debates about it, there would be two or three nights about the Herald of Truth and two or three with one of the orphan homes named in the proposition.

The first public debate on these issues was in 1954 in Indianapolis, Indiana between W. L. Totty and Charles A. Holt. The first night, W. L. Totty defended the scriptural right of churches to support colleges, then there were two nights devoted to the Herald of Truth and two nights to the orphan home question. It did not take long for preachers who opposed the sponsoring church arrangement to be characterized as "anti-cooperation" and those who opposed church support of the orphan institutions to be dubbed "anti-orphan." In some of the debates emotional arguments were made to the effect that a mean old anti preacher would let a little orphan starve before he would help him, or if one was struck by a car in front of the church building, he would not even let the church phone be used to call an ambulance. N. B. Hardeman, of *Hardeman Tabernacle Sermons* fame as well as having his name connected with Freed-

Hardeman College, wrote in the *Gospel Advocate* that the church support of colleges and orphan homes "stands or falls together."

As a young preacher, I had to sort all of this out and decide where I would stand. After I moved to Atlanta, Georgia, my wife and I decided to attend the Holt-Totty debate in Indianapolis. Before that event, Franklin T. Puckett urged me to read the *Otey-Briney Debate* which took place in Louisville, Kentucky in 1908. I took his advice. I did not have to listen to W. L. Totty very long until I saw the parallels between J. B. Briney's arguments to defend church supported missionary societies and those made by Totty to defend the practices in his propositions for debate. In 1956 I attended the Tant-Harper Debate in Abilene, Texas and heard E. R. Harper do the same thing in his defense of Herald of Truth. In addition, the controversies being aired about all these issues in the *Firm Foundation, Gospel Advocate,* and *Gospel Gaurdian* really helped me during those hectic years. When I took my Bible and followed the arguments being made, pro and con, it was not hard for me to see where the truth was found. Standing for the truth had a price tag on it. In the mid-fifties an older, well known preacher, wrote me and said that, if I continued to "follow after the antis," my influence would be destroyed and there would be no place for me to preach. I received a few questionnaires as to where I stood on the Herald of Truth and orphan homes. When my answers did not please those who sent them, then some meetings were cancelled, including some places where I had been at least twice and where we had baptized a number of people. But the price was small for this young preacher compared to that which was exacted against men like Roy E. Cogdill, Yater Tant, Franklin T. Puckett, Luther Blackmen, James W. Adams, Hoyt Houchen, James R. Cope, and a long list of worthies who were willing to "buy the truth and sell it not."

The cost was great in terms of family and personal friendships. The congregation where my father had served as an elder in Virginia and in which I had received much encouragement to preach during my teen years, wound up supporting the institutional movement. Some family members remained there. My best friend decided to attend David Lipscomb College and we drifted apart. Preachers we had come to love and respect ended up on the other side. Tears were shed. Hearts were broken. Those who have thought and said, that the division could have been averted had brethren just been sweet and kind to each other have been sadly misinformed. No, there were real, live issues at stake. The very nature, work, and organization of the church for which our Lord died were on the line. Lifelong friends and comrades in arms found themselves at opposite tables during debates. Many of those who contended for the sponsoring church and church supported institutions never dreamed how far some would take their arguments. Today, there are a small number of men who are trying to turn back the tsunami generated by the "where there is no pattern" arguments of the 1950's and 1960's. Some of them are publishing very good material, which would have been received with open arms years ago by the *Gospel Guardian, The Preceptor, Searching The Scriptures,* or *Truth Magazine*. But these men are also being called "antis" and they are decidedly in the minority. If they would only apply what they are saying to the principle of the sponsoring church and the church support of private organizations, we could strike hands and fight side by side in contending for the "old paths."

Chapter 5

Local Preaching

During the years at Florida Christian College, I was blessed in having a place to preach on Sundays. In my first and third year I spoke at Cortez. The church there was largely the result of work done by Byron Connely and W. A. Cameron who conducted meetings (many of them in tents) all over the state of Florida. The number of members fluctuated over the years and in 1948-49 had about twenty-five in attendance. There were only two men in the number and one of them led singing. The church had been kept alive by godly women who refused to give up. We were able to baptize some and a few were restored. Winter visitors (called "snowbirds" by the locals) helped attendance as they came to the Bradenton and Anna Maria Island area.

Preaching at Lake Wales was interesting work. The church also numbered about twenty-five. My friend, Roy Lanier, Jr., had preached for them during the school year and introduced them to me. They invited me to spend the summer with them. They paid me $50 a week and I stayed in a large boarding house. I made friends with the husband of a faithful member who was an excellent fisherman. He worked as a guide to snowbird fishermen and knew where to go to fish. We spent the day fishing a number of times and I had a chance to talk with him about the Bible and his soul. Before the summer was over, we had Arley Moore to come for a meeting and my friend was baptized along with nine others. Some of the others I met in an interesting way. After having Sunday dinner with a family which took care of a large cattle ranch and some citrus groves, I was passing by a house where there were some young people on the porch and one of the boys was playing a guitar. I stopped and asked if I could listen awhile. Finally, the boy noticed that I was harmonizing on some of his songs and asked "Do you play?" I thought he would never ask! "A little," I said. He handed me the guitar and after a few numbers, he said, "Who are you? What do you do?" I think they were surprised when I told them. We had a good visit and when leaving, I invited them to come hear me preach. To my surprised most of them did. Some of them were among those baptized in the meeting. I continued to preach there during the school year of 1949-50.

Palmetto, Florida

During my senior year at college, I was invited to preach at Palmetto while they were between preachers. The church numbered 80-90. After a few weeks, they asked if I would move there and work with them full time when I finished school. We agreed to do so. For the rest of the school term we drove down to Palmetto every Sunday and Wednesday night. In April, 1953, one of the two elders died suddenly. That left the church without elders. In a few months another man was appointed and the former elder agreed to serve again. For some reason we did not seem to be on the same page. We had a Sunday morning radio program on which I preached on first principles and drew a line between the church revealed in the New Testament and denominationalism. I was called in and advised to tone it down. In the local preaching I spent much time addressing the church about how to grow and seeking to correct some worldliness among the members. Again I was called in and advised to let up. It is altogether likely that, as a young preacher, I did not always use the best judgment but, to this day, I am convinced that what was being preached was the truth. Bobbie and I talked it over and decided that, since we seemed to be at cross purposes, it would be best if I resigned. I called the elders aside on a Wednesday night and told them that I thought it would be best for them and for me to make a change and that I was giving them the three months notice we had agreed to when I came.

Much to my surprise, the following Sunday, after everyone else had left, the elders followed me to our car and told me they had secured another preacher who would begin the following Sunday and that we were to vacate the house (which the church owned) within the week. I reminded them of the three months agreement we had made, told them that I did not have any place to go, and would need a little time to arrange that. The newer elder was the spokesman and he became very agitated and informed me in no uncertain terms that I was to be out of that house in a week and that I would not be allowed back in the pulpit, not even to say goodbye to the congregation. By then, Bobbie was in tears. I said that I would not be out of the house in a week and that if they wanted to come and move our things out in the yard to feel free to do so and we would not try to stop them. But I also promised them that when brethren drove by and saw our furniture in the yard and asked what was going on, that I would tell them to ask the elders to explain it to them. When we were not at services that night (we attended service in Bradenton), brethren began asking questions.

We made a trip to Tampa to talk with James P. Miller (who had known Bobbie most of her life) and seek his advice. Some had approached me about starting another congregation. Brother Miller urged me not to "touch that with a ten foot pole." He said, "You are young and can move on, but those folks live there and such a division would take fifty years to heal if it ever does." He promised to help us find another place to work. And he did just that. We had a summer to spend with no steady income and we alternated between time with our families in Virginia and Kentucky. A few preaching appointments opened up and a couple of gospel meetings were held. Looking back, that is the roughest treatment I ever had in local work. I learned from it and the church survived. After we left, the brethren insisted that the elders make correction. They wrote me a very nice letter (which I have kept) in which they apologized and stated that I had preached the truth and that they commended my manner of life. I have been invited twice for meetings there since that time.

Glenwood Hills in Decatur, Georgia
True to his word, James P. Miller contacted the church at Glenwood Hills in a suburb of Atlanta and recommended us for the work. So in September, 1954, we moved to Georgia. Atlanta then was a sleeping giant of 600,000 people. They were in the early stages of growth and expansion which has made it a huge metropolitan area. Many businesses were establishing headquarters there and subdivisions were being built all over the red clay hills of surrounding counties. It was a good time for the church to grow. People were pulling up roots, starting fresh in a new place, looking for new friends and many were open to the gospel. I had spent one month, two years before that, preaching at West End in Atlanta while J. Ed Nowlin was away in meetings. I liked the area and welcomed the opportunity. We got off to a rocky start. The previous preacher was much loved. The church had no elders and, in the first few monthly business meetings, we were all reminded again and again about "what John would have done." Finally, I asked for the floor and said, "John decided to move and you invited me to preach here. I am not John; I'll do the best I can, if you will help me." We heard no about "what John would do." Through the years, I have dreaded business meetings. In the first place, many of them are misnamed when the word

"business" is associated with them. Often an hour is spent on something which could be dealt with in five minutes. You can have peaceful, orderly meetings until all at once, out of the blue, someone "drops a clod in the churn" (as Tennessee Ernie Ford used to say) and

Glenwood Hills church building in Decatur, Georgia (1955).

bedlam follows. In one such meeting at Glenwood Hills, the discussion was becoming overheated when I asked if I could speak. The chairman said, "Please do." I said, "Brethren, I think we ought to get down on our knees and pray and I will lead the prayer, since I am not angry." You could have heard a pin drop and after the prayer, we had a peaceful meeting. There is no sense in brethren acting like heathens.

That became a very fruitful work. Many moved into the area and placed membership, some of them were very good workers. We restored the erring, withdrew from the unrepentant, and baptized a good many people. We had lots of home studies resulting in conversions. Most of the women did not work outside the home and some of them were zealous to arrange studies with neighbors. The cultural changes which have taken wives and mothers into the work place have affected evangelism and slowed the growth of many congregations. During those three years, we grew to 160-170, appointed two elders, started a radio program, and developed talent within the congregation. I preached in a number of meetings, some nearby but others more distant. Some thought I was gone too much. We made close friends which remain to this day "though some are fallen asleep."

During this time, with the urging of two sisters who were driving forty miles from Covington to worship, we began the work in Covington. We advertised in the local paper and began meeting in the American Legion Hall on Sunday afternoons. We rounded up some unfaithful members, restored them, baptized others, and got the work off the ground. I drove down and preached for about a year. A number of Glenwood members attended and helped in many ways.

Some land was secured and many Saturdays were spent with Glenwood brethren working with Covington folks to put up a building. Ladies there would bring our lunch. We got it done and in May, 1955, I held the first meeting in the new building. The church has grown a great deal and is now relocated in a very commodious meeting house and doing much good work. In 2005, I was invited to preach for them on the Sunday which marked the fiftieth year since we had that first meeting in the Legion Hall.

For one year of the time we were at Glenwood Hills, I spoke five times every Sunday. We had a thirty-minute radio program on Sunday morning (which was done live), then a Bible class and sermon at Glenwood Hills, then the forty mile trip to Covington and back, and then another service at six that evening. But those were good years and I yet regard them as among the most fruitful local works with which we have had a part.

But those were also critical years in terms of the growing storm involving institutionalism. After attending the Holt-Totty debate in 1954, I began to write articles in the local bulletin about these issues. That did not set well with some other local preachers who were leaning the other way. We could get together for lunch and have amicable discussions, and some of them talked a pretty good fight. But they did not preach on it or write anything in their bulletins. They had men for meetings who were clearly liberal in sentiment and practice. Privately, a few told me they agreed with what I was saying but they wished I would back off and let it rest. We had Yater Tant twice for meetings and that upset some in the area since he was editor of the *Gospel Guardian*. Some, who came to hear him, were surprised at his pleasant spirit and reasonableness. In 1955 we had Foy E. Wallace, Jr. for a memorable meeting.

He did some of the best expository preaching I had ever heard. One night he spoke on the organization and work of the church. He zeroed in on the sponsoring church and laid three charges against it. First, sponsoring elders were "ecumenical elders," or brotherhood elders, overseeing work which belonged to each contributing church. He said the practice was contrary to Acts 20:28 and 1 Peter 5:2 and that they were overseeing more than "the flock of God among them." Second, he said they were practicing "religious feudalism" and that the sponsoring elders were the "barons" while the contributing churches were the "serfs." It violated the equality of churches. Third, he charged that the practice constituted a "chain" of churches, sort of "Piggly Wiggly churches of Christ." For those who don't remember, Piggly Wiggly was a chain of grocery stores in the south and southwest. In the audience that night was the area representative for the Herald of Truth and one of the elders where he preached. They were not pleased. During that eight day meeting, the elders requested that, on the second Sunday afternoon, he speak on the book of Revelation giving an overview. He had done so much work refuting premillennialism and opposing their erroneous views especially on chapter 20, that we were all interested in what he would say. We began at 3 P.M., had prayer, and I led one song. He spoke until 6 P.M. Oddly, I led for an invitation, "Why Do You Wait Dear Brother?" But nobody left. He spent the first hour discussing the date of the book and giving his reasons for accepting the early date, before the destruction of Jerusalem in A.D. 70. At the time, I thought he made a good case, but through the years since, I have had difficulty with several passages in the book assuming that early date, plus what I consider a preponderance of external evidence for a date near the end of the first century. He did not preach one sermon which was less than an hour and twenty minutes. But we had the house full from night to night, the audience sensed the rare treat we were having and, if anyone complained about the length of the sermons, I don't recall it. We have become a spoiled people who want it cut and dried, neatly packaged, brightly adorned with stories and snappy one-liners, and quickly delivered. The week was pleasant for me personally. Sister Wallace was sick and he took care of her in a motel. For that reason he did not accept invitations for meals. But he invited me to eat breakfast with him at the motel restaurant several times. He took one afternoon and went with me to my study at the building. He looked over my books, said I had a "good start" and recommended several books I needed to get as soon as finances permitted. I took his advice and have never been sorry, especially with the five volume set of Horne's *Introduction to the Scriptures*. As we walked by the platform, I stopped to clean off the chalk board and he said, "You know, Connie, if a preacher doesn't get a little chalk dust on his coattail, he is not too solid anyhow." I think about that when I preach in buildings in which you are out of luck if you don't have a PowerPoint presentation to go with your sermon. I have never had a piece of chalk to let me down.

Brother Wallace was an enigma to me, as well as to some others. His militance in the premillennial controversy sorely displeased some of the writers and readers of the *Gospel Advocate*. He was editor of that journal in the early to mid-1930's.

In the late 1930's he began the *Bible Banner* in which he militantly opposed church support of the colleges. He had a very intense exchange in the *Advocate* with N. B. Hardeman over that very issue in the late 1940's. Influential men who were leading churches toward institutionalism were uncomfortable with him. His heavy artillery aimed at the sponsoring church arrangement certainly did not endear him to them. In 1962, when we lived at Newbern, Tennessee, he came through on his way to Hot Springs, Arkansas where he often took sister Wallace for the warm springs baths. He called me and invited me to join them for lunch in Dyersburg. I had with me a folder of bulletins from liberal churches announcing all sorts of social activities from movies to greased pig chases to "Who can get the most grapes in his mouth?" contests. He looked at some of it and said, "I am as much opposed to that as you are." But he had had some personal differences with Roy Cogdill and Yater Tant. Since his son, William, agreed with Tant and Cogdill, an estrangement was created which lasted many years. I understand that before his death, he and William met and resolved their differences. I know for a fact that both Tant and Cogdill grieved over the matter and tried to do what they could to solve it, but without success. The last few years of his life, brother Wallace was cut off from non-institutional brethren and was used by some churches which were institutionally minded but which had not gone quite as far as the majority had. Many of the members of these churches did not appreciate the monumental work he had done in opposing premillennial error which, if unchecked, would have led churches into denominationalism. It is sad to me that, in his latter years, he found himself circulating among those who did not really appreciate what he had done in earlier years and alienated from those who did.

Let me get back to Glenwood Hills in Atlanta. When all the smoke had settled, the only church in that area which stood clearly opposed to institutionalism was Glenwood Hills. The other faithful churches now in that area owe their existence in large part to the stand that was taken there. In time, Glenwood Hills became a high crime area and the church relocated near Stone Mountain. That work has since disbanded and the members scattered to other congregations.

It was while living and working at Glenwood Hills that Bobbie and I decided to go to Norway to try to start the work. The brethren were supportive of our plans though genuinely sad to see us leave. The final service before our departure was choked with emotion. W. F. Dudley, one of the elders, led the singing that night and, in view of the trials we might face in a foreign country in establishing a church there, he led the song "Ready to Suffer" right before the sermon. I knew that, if I could not somehow relieve the tension and emotion we all felt, I would not be able to get through my last sermon there. So I said,

"Now here I thought brother Dudley was my friend, but right before I got up to preach, he chose 'Ready to Suffer'. Is my preaching all that painful?" We all had a good laugh, the tension was broken and I was able to speak without breaking down.

First Debate

It was while preaching at Glenwood Hills that I had my first public debate. I met J. H. Payne of Porterdale, Georgia (near Covington) in a four night debate conducted in a high school auditorium in Decatur. He preached for the United Pentecostals, sometimes called the "Oneness Holiness" Church. He had already had a few debates and was a good speaker. When I expressed some misgivings to Franklin T. Puckett as to whether or not I could make an adequate defense and not have the truth suffer, brother Puckett reassured me. He said, "You have a great advantage over Payne. You have the truth and he does not."

The first two nights we discussed the number of persons in the Godhead. He contended that God has manifested Himself as the Father in the Old Testament, as the Son while Jesus was on earth, and now as the Holy Spirit. He read passages from Isaiah where the idea of one God is contrasted to polytheism. He said Jesus is the only person in the Godhead and that baptism must be in His name only. He likened the Godhead to an egg. He had a chart with a cutaway picture of an egg identifying the shell, the white, and the yolk. He said it was all one egg and you could not separate it. The second night, I had Bobbie to separate me an egg. In one container I had the shell, in another the white and in another the yolk. I thanked him for the argument which perfectly illustrated my position. I held up the three containers and said, "Let me introduce you to egg, the shell; egg, the white; and egg, the yolk. While the three are separate entities, they all have the nature of egg. You see it is like God the Father, God the Son, and God the Holy Spirit. They are three distinct personalities yet all share the nature of Deity as opposed to humanity."

The last two nights we discussed miraculous divine healing. I affirmed that this had ceased and he argued that it continued. He made an argument from Mark 16:17-18 and chided me for believing and preaching verse 16 but not the rest of it. He put great emphasis on "they shall lay hands on the sick and they shall recover." I pointed out that verses 19-20 showed the purpose of the gifts in confirming the word as it was being revealed and argued from 1 Corinthians 13:8-13 that miracles had now confirmed the word and had ceased. Jere Frost, who then preached at Chamblee, on the northeast side of Atlanta, moderated for me and was great help.

We decided to test Mr. Payne on Mark 16:17-18. It also says, "If you drink any deadly thing, it will not hurt you." I brought a quart bottle of Roman Cleanser Bleach and challenged him to take a good drink of it. I asked Jere what we would do if he was foolish enough to drink some of it. He assured me that the man was not about to do that. I trusted Jere and he was right. He argued that "a wicked and adulterous generation seeks after a sign" and that we were "tempting God." I replied that we had no doubt about what God could do, but that *he* was the one we doubted. We both pressed our points but maintained good humor throughout.

The debate was very well attended by both members of the church and Pentecostals and good order prevailed. The best debater for the United Pentecostal Church for many years was D. L. Welch of Pensacola, Florida. He debated a good many of our brethren. After his death, J. H. Payne became their best one. Alexander Campbell once said that a week of debating was worth a year of preaching in terms of how much study and preparation is involved. He was pretty close to the truth on that. Some have negative feelings about debates. Truth be told, some debates have done harm either because the one defending the truth was not well prepared and the truth suffered, or else did not conduct himself as a Christian should. But we had the opportunity to preach the truth to many more Pentecostals than we could have reached in ten gospel meetings, if at all.

Chapter 6

Preaching in the Land of the Midnight Sun

"Who put that bee in your bonnet to go across the ocean and preach?" That question was put to me by John T. Lewis in Birmingham, Alabama when Marshall E. Patton and I went to visit. For all his gruff speech at times, brother Lewis had a very tender heart. He listened to my answer, gave me some good advice and, before we left, he had sister Lewis to write a check for $100 to help on our travel expenses to Norway.

Before Bobbie and I married, we talked about spending some part of our lives preaching in another country. In 1956 we began seriously considering that desire. We had been married for six years and had no children. We had explored adoption and had even contacted two of the orphan homes run by brethren. We were surprised to learn that many of the children were not actually orphans and were not eligible for adoption. We decided that we could not use children as an excuse to keep from going over seas. In our private home devotionals we had read together W. W. Otey's book *The Tree of Life Lost and Regained*. There was a chapter in it on Abraham and his faith in leaving his country and kindred. Somehow, that stirred up our hearts and emboldened us to seriously consider plans to preach in another land. We considered going to Australia since there would be no language barrier (well, maybe not much), but there were some congregations already there and we really wanted to go where there was no work established. We read a survey report of Scandinavia in one of the papers and became intensely interested in what was said about Norway. We went to the library and began to read all we could find about that land of the midnight sun. We decided to go to Bergen, the second largest city and the largest on the west coast, a city then of about 150,000. We took what steps we could to start working on the language.

We set a departure date in September, 1957. Bobbie took a job at Rich's Department Store in downtown Atlanta to help us pay off all our debts. I began writing letters to seek support. Very few of those letters were ever acknowledged. But finally in the late spring of 1957, with the help of Yater Tant and others, I was able to work out an itinerary to visit a number of congregations and speak directly about the work we proposed to do and ask for support. Reactions from those we visited were mixed. Some were highly interested and others were more curious than anything else. Some thought we had plenty of work to do in our own country, and, of course, that was true. Some asked if a soul saved in Georgia was not as valuable as one in Norway. But to my mind the issue was clear. As the song goes, "The Blessed Gospel is For All." I often quoted the line in that song, "Say not the heathen are at home, Beyond we have no call." At that time 7% of the world's population lived in the United States while more than 90% of gospel preachers were working among that 7%. The odds were not even. In the Great Commission Jesus had charged the apostles to "go . . . teach all nations" and then "teach them to observe all things I have commanded you" (Matt. 28:18-20). One thing he had clearly commanded them was "go teach all nations."

I found some of the concepts of some brethren interesting. They viewed me as aspiring to be a "missionary." In Georgia I was an evangelist, a preacher, but if I went to Norway that would make me a "missionary." I informed all who would listen that I would be doing in Norway the same thing we were doing in Georgia, "the work of an evangelist." I had always, and still do, shy away from the word "missionary." I habitually refer to Paul's journeys as his "preaching trips." The word "missionary" conjures up the idea of going to establish "missions." We were going to establish a church of the Lord in Bergen, Norway which would not be tied to some "mother church" or ecclesiastical organization.

We were trying to raise $420 a month plus travel expenses. Of course, U.S. dollars were worth far more then than they are now. There was another problem, though. While all the lines had not been drawn among brethren over the sponsoring church, some of them had been drawn. At each place I spoke, it was made clear that I would not be working under a sponsoring church, that all support would be sent directly to me, and that a report would be sent monthly to each supporting congregation. I reminded them that, while there was controversy over the sponsoring church, everybody agreed that it was scriptural for a church, or for churches, to send support directly to a preacher in the field (2 Cor. 11:8; Phil. 4:15-16). Two congregations which agreed to help support us definitely got off the fence on the liberal side after we went to Norway and after one year, and without notice, dropped our support. Thankfully we were able to replace it.

The road trip to finalize support lasted about three weeks during which I visited churches in Alabama, Tennessee, Missouri, Kentucky, and Ohio. There were twelve congregations which agreed to support us monthly. The amounts ranged from $10 a month to $50 a month. Most of them were very prompt in what they sent, while a couple of places were slow at times. Brethren do not always appreciate what it is like to be in a distant place and dependent on the mail to bring the means of your livelihood. As a foreigner, I was not allowed to work for wages. Out of our $420 a month, we had to rent a place to live and provide a good part of the expense of the work that had to be done. We never had a "work fund." Some individuals at times helped with some special needs.

The Best Laid Plans

The last stop on my fund raising trip was in Akron, Ohio. All of our support had been promised except $50 a month. After speaking at Southeast in Akron on Sunday, they agreed to take up that amount. I called Bobbie to tell her the good news and to say that I was heading home. She seemed pleased but hesitant. She said, "I have something to tell you when you get home." "What is it?" I wanted to know. She said, "I think I am pregnant." "Are you sure?" I asked. "Pretty sure," she said. I told her we could put our travel plans on hold until after the baby came but she wanted to wait and think it through. Then she said something I will never forget. "Do you remember that chapter in brother Otey's book about Abraham? Well, maybe the Lord is trying to see if our faith is real." I drove home to Georgia with a confusion of thoughts. If we delayed our plans, would all of the brethren understand and still be willing to support us? Would it be a lack of faith on our part if we did not go or had to delay plans? What if something went wrong? We would be in another country far removed from family and friends. Bobbie was an only child and, if something went wrong, how could I ever face her parents again? When I got home, we had some long talks about it. She, typically, had done her homework on medical facilities in Bergen. We prayed that we would make the right decision. Finally, she said, "You know, babies are born every day in Norway, they have modern medical facilities, and I don't see why we should not go ahead with our plans." At the time, I thought her faith was much stronger than mine. So, we proceeded with plans. She continued to work at Rich's for a few more weeks. We made arrangements to sell furniture (and store special things such as china and silver, given to us as wedding presents). We had a 1956 Desoto (made by Chrysler) which we had bought new. It was the nicest car we had driven up to that time. I sold it to a brother in Rome, Georgia and after paying off what we owed on it, cleared $300. We hoped we could find a good, used car in Norway. Fat chance!

Not only was Bobbie's mother unhappy with our decision (and looking back, I understand her anxiety much better than I did then), but my mother was also very unhappy (to put it mildly) with our plans. My father called me and asked if I could come to Virginia for a couple of days and talk with them about it. In those days, we wrote letters and waited for answers. Telephone calls were rare for us, so I knew this was urgent. My mother was worried about how cold it was in Norway (one third of the country was in the Arctic Circle). She was concerned for Bobbie and the baby. How was I going to talk to the people since I did not speak the language? Were there not any more lost souls in Georgia? I pointed out that there were brethren in Georgia who could carry on the work without us, but nobody, where we were going, to do that. Then she asked, "Why does it have to be you?" I answered, "Why not me?" Then she hit me with a hard question. "What if Grandmammy dies and you can't get home?" When I talked to Grandmammy, she told me to go on and preach the gospel and do all the good I could and that, if we did not get to see each other again in Virginia, we would meet on the other side. Several years later when we were in Virginia for a visit, my mother and I were alone on the porch when she brought up that subject and apologized for her efforts to hinder us from going to Norway. She said, "The real truth is, I just did not want my baby boy across the ocean. But I will promise you that I will never again try to keep you from going anywhere in the world you think you need to go to preach." And she kept her word.

An older couple at Glenwood Hills, the W. B. Kickliters, decided to go with us to Bergen and stay three months so they could help us get settled. What a blessing that was. He was an accountant and his work was slow in the fall. Then a few weeks before we were to set sail, Mary Russell, the widow of the elder who died when we were in Palmetto, Florida, called and asked if she could be of any help if she went and stayed a few months. We were elated to have her go with us. She stayed eight months and was great help, especially after the baby was born.

We were to travel to Norway by ship, the SS Oslofjord, a vessel that carried six hundred passengers and a crew of two hundred. We crated things we thought we would need, including most of my library (and, of course, my guitar). We were allowed so many pounds of cargo with the price of each ticket. But we had seven pieces of luggage just for Bobbie and me. She had one suitcase full of baby clothes and supplies which had been given to her in a shower in Virginia. We all met at the Taft Hotel in New York City where we spent the night before sailing the next day for the seven day voyage. We talked excitedly about our plans and prayed earnestly for those we were leaving behind, for our own safety, for the healthy arrival of our baby, and, above all, that God would open doors for us to teach His word and lead souls to Christ.

When we arrived by taxi at the hotel, I was introduced to different manners than what we were accustomed to in Atlanta. The driver unloaded our seven pieces of luggage and I gave him what I thought was a good tip. I had on a Stetson hat which was a gift from my mother-in-law, and he looked me up and down and said, "Come on, Tex, you can do better than that. Man, you got seven bags here!"

Before the ship sailed the next morning, they played the Norwegian national anthem and then they played the Star Spangled Banner. We all stood with tears streaming down our faces and I vowed that, if they played it again, I would just have to get off that ship. As we left the harbor, we passed by the Statue of Liberty and I wondered if we would ever see that proud lady again.

The voyage was uneventful except for two days of rough seas in the north Atlantic. The Kickliters got seasick. Bobbie had some rough moments. As long as we were lying down, we did all right. I did not lose my victuals, but I did miss a few trips to the dining room. There was a passenger talent show one night and I signed up. I borrowed a guitar from one of the band members and asked the bass player to back me up. I picked and sang "Sleepin' at the Foot of the Bed," an old Jimmy Dickens tune, and received an encore. I did a soft ballad. It was nice to win the contest. On the Lord's Day, the five of us worshipped in our cabin. We *were* the church on that ship. We sang, prayed, I taught a Bible lesson, and brother Kickliter served the Lord's Supper with appropriate remarks. We asked him to hold our contribution until we could start an account in a bank in Bergen and to serve as treasurer until they had to return to the states in November.

Arrival

As we approached the rocky coast of western Norway, we were filled with excitement, yet suddenly awed to think of what a task we had undertaken. As we slipped through the fjord toward the pier in Bergen, we began to see brightly colored houses with patches of green pastures. Bergen is situated at the foot of several mountains with houses extending up the sides.

After we docked, we had to clear customs. We had to open some of our baggage. When Bobbie opened the suitcase with all the baby clothes, the customs officer said, "What is this?" She said, "Baby clothes." He looked around and said, "Where is baby?" She patted her enlarged stomach, he turned red, muttered something which we did not understand (it is probably just as well), and then waved us through.

Now we had to leave the safety of the ship to hail a taxi to go to the Terminus Hotel where we had a reservation for one week. We hoped by then we could locate a place to rent. How naïve we were. We were all eyes as we drove through this strange city with its curious mixture of the very old and the very new.

After getting our baggage settled in our rooms, we were anxious to get out and see what was nearby. It was raining, as it often is in Bergen that time of year. We found umbrellas and began to walk toward the central area of the city. We were an odd assortment and became the object of much staring from the locals. Brother Kickliter was short and stout (there were not many stout men in Bergen then); Sister Kickliter had been injured in an automobile accident some years before, had a bad hip, and walked with a limp; Bobbie was obviously expecting. Mary Russell had come from Florida with a deep tan which contrasted with her white, cashmere coat. All three women wore white socks over their hose to keep their feet warm. As for me, I was the only man in Bergen with a light grey, eight gallon Stetson hat. Folks, we were a sight to behold in Bergen, Norway in 1957! People would meet us, look us up and down, and then turn around and stare at us after we had passed. I know, because I turned around a couple of times to see. Lesson number one: we had to do something about our wardrobe.

Providence at Work

The next morning, Mary Russell and I set out to buy a used car. The hotel manager had already told us housing was scarce. That was not encouraging but it was factual. He told us of a used car dealer down near the docks. We took a taxi to shop for a car. When we arrived, there was not a car on the lot which we were sure would even make it off the lot. They were all *very used cars*. I only had a limited amount to spend but did not want to buy trouble. We were having trouble communicating with the dealer. He motioned for us to come into his office and said something which meant, "Wait a moment." He phoned someone

Bergen, Norway (1957).

and handed me the phone. The voice on line was an attorney who also owned an interest in the Opel dealership in town. An Opel is not a piece of jewelry, but a four-cylinder car made by General Motors in Germany. He spoke English very well and after explaining to him our situation, he gave me the address of his office and invited us to come and said he would try to help us. The taxi driver easily found the address and we were soon in his nicely furnished office. On the way there, Mary Russell offered to finance a new car for us and said we could make payments to her and use what I had saved for a down payment. The attorney was very kind and in time we became friends. He was curious as to why we had come to Norway and listened with interest. He not only helped us buy a car (which took one month to complete), but also offered to write some newspaper ads for us seeking a place to live, and to go with us and help in the transaction should something become available. He recommended a bank. He also made us a copy of the "dissenter laws" for religions in Norway, other than the Lutheran Church, which was the state religion. He asked if we planned to study the language and I assured him that we did. He said he had a friend who ran Bergen's Sprog Skole, a language school. He called his friend and handed me the phone. Right then and there, we made arrangements for three classes a week, starting the very next morning. All of these things fell into place the first day after arrival. We could hardly wait to get back to the hotel and tell the others.

Our week in the hotel turned into a month and was becoming expensive. During that time we worshipped in our hotel room. We found a meeting room we could afford in the Victoria Hotel which would seat 40-50 people. This hotel did not serve alcohol, had a good name among religious people, and the Temperance League held meetings there. We were able to rent it twice on Sundays and for Wednesday nights as well as for a few special meetings. In the meantime, Mr. Haake, who ran the language school, had taken a liking to us and we had some interesting discussions. He asked if I would agree to an interview with the religion editor of Bergen's *Tidende*, the largest newspaper on Norway's west coast. I had no idea what he might say about us, but also knew that somehow people needed to know we were there and why. I readily agreed and Mr. Haake set up the meeting. The man was very nice but asked pointed questions about the history and nature of the church, how we differed from other groups, and what our objectives were in Bergen. He called in a photographer to make my picture to run with the article. I did not know what to expect. The article appeared in a Friday edition which was not only widely read in Bergen, but in the villages on the fjords of western Norway. The piece appeared on the front page of the second section of the paper and covered half a page. To my surprise, he treated us fairly, quoted me accurately, and told readers to watch for advertisements as to when and where our meetings would begin. Even Mr. Haake was surprised at how well we were treated.

Mr. Erland, our lawyer friend, helped us to secure a house halfway up Mt. Floyen overlooking the city. The owner's son lived in the basement which had its own private entrance. We had the top two floors. Upstairs, there were three rooms, two of which we used for bedrooms and one for my study. On the first floor there was a large living room, dining room, bedroom, kitchen, and bath. The owner was moving to California and wanted the rent paid in dollars. The rent was $70 a month. We were all glad to get out of the hotel and get settled and do our own cooking. Shopping for groceries was another adjustment. You bought meat from a meat shop (where else?), bread from a bakery, fish, fruit, and vegetables from the open market on the wharf, and canned goods and other supplies from the grocer. It took awhile to shop. Bobbie's vocabulary quickly centered around words for our domestic world while mine involved other things.

We began public meetings in October, 1957, with a gospel meeting (Sunday-Friday) at the Victoria Hotel. We advertised this, with the subjects, in three newspapers. We hired an interpreter from the language school, rented earphones and a tape recorder from an electronics store, and were ready to get something going. We ran lines from the back of the tape recorder to these plastic earphones which were plugged in under the seats. Those who could not speak English could listen to the interpreter through the earphones. The interpreter spoke softly into a microphone and would be finished with a sentence almost as soon as I was. It worked pretty well. I must say that we were on edge about that first meeting on Sunday morning. Would anyone come? Had it all been in vain? Well, besides the five of us, eight people came, all of whom had read the interview in the newspaper and cut it out and kept it awaiting announcement of our first service. Some of those first visitors continued to come and in time two of them were baptized. Attendance during the meeting included six to twelve visitors nightly. Some came out of curiosity and only appeared once or twice. Others came off and on the whole time we were there but never obeyed the gospel. But we had made a start. On Thursday night I spoke on the "Establishment of the Church." In the course of it, I pointed out that this fulfilled the prophecies about the establishment of the kingdom. At the end of my sermon, a man stood up near the back of the room and said he did not believe the kingdom had yet been established and that he wondered if I would be willing to publicly debate the issue. I told him he had come to the right place and that seemed to surprise him. It turned out that he was the leader in Bergen of the Christadelphians. They were a small group and were supported by some of their folks in England. I went to his home to discuss arrangements and was cordially received. He said he did not think his English was adequate to debate with me in that language and wondered if I would meet one of their representatives from Yorkshire, England. I assured him I would. This led to a correspondence with A. D. Norris, then secretary of the movement and who had written several books on their doctrine. We set a date during the first week of January, rented a large room at the library and began to make plans. Cecil Willis had two of the books by Norris and sent them to me. Len Channing, a preacher in England, sent me valuable books by David King, a contemporary of A. Campbell, on the history of that movement. I had good ammunition of my own, and began to make ready. There was one major problem. Our baby was due sometime in late December. But the prospect of a debate and making new contacts was too great an opportunity to pass up. Looking back, I see the hand of God opening doors of opportunity and answering prayers. Yes, I believe in the providence of God.

Who Is the Foreigner?

We had to make major adjustments to social and business practices. It took ten days to get our dry cleaning back. I had to go to three different tellers at the bank to make a deposit. I had to have a notarized statement witnessed by our attorney friend to get my own cancelled checks back. They made a solemn ceremony out of it. I solemnly agreed to take full responsibility for receipt of my own cancelled checks. At home we enjoyed talking about what strange things had happened to us that day. But after we had been there about three months, we were listening to the Armed Forces Radio Network from Stuttgart, Germany and they ran a public service announcement by Tennessee Ernie Ford aimed at American service families. He said, "Peapickers, when you're in the other fellers country, *you're* the furrener." That hit me like a bolt out of the blue. Those people we had been laughing about were at home. *We* were the foreigners. That probably helped me adjust about as much as anything could. In fact, by the summer I had come to be ashamed of the behavior of some American tourists who were bossy, rude, and superior acting. When you and your family go to another country, or even a different part of your own country, you would do well to go to the library, read something of the customs and history of the area, and, if you are going to live there, try to fit into the local scenery as much as you can without violating some divine principle.

Before the Kickliters returned, we were all invited into the home of a Methodist lady who had attended several of our meetings. She became a very good friend to us. This was our first invitation into a real Norwegian home. It was a very pleasant evening. Sister Kickliter wanted to make a good impression and learned to say a few things in Norwegian such as "Good evening," "Thanks for inviting us," "That was delicious." As we were leaving she said with real emphasis "Tusen takk for ingenting." Our hosts appeared startled at first, but recovered quickly. I nearly fainted. What she meant to say was "Tusen takk for alleting" (a thousand thanks for everything). What she actually said was, "A thousand thanks for nothing." She was so proud of her language skills that none of us had the heart to tell her what she had said and later we had a good laugh with the family of the host and hostess about it.

Speaking of language, I worked hard to learn enough to preach in Norwegian. If I had stayed there the rest of my life, I would have spoken it with a southern accent. But after six months, I was able largely to read a manuscript at one service a week. Mr. Haake corrected my grammar and helped me with inflections. After a few more weeks, I was able to speak from a rather full outline.

Then the last year we were there, I could preach from a brief outline. Norwegian is rooted in German and is not a very complicated language. Until I was able to speak freely, we used an interpreter.

A Child Is Born

On a cold Saturday morning, Bobbie told me it was time for her to go to the hospital. A noted gynecologist had been recommended to us by her doctor in Atlanta. He had invented some surgical tools which made him well known internationally. But he was a known Communist and our government had denied him entry into our country for a medical conference. But he was very kind to Bobbie. At that time in Norway, unless there were complications with a birth, professional midwives delivered the babies. She was taken to a woman's hospital. I was not allowed to stay. They told me they would keep me informed and I could come at regular visiting hours after the baby was born. She was in labor all that day and night. I had to preach on Sunday morning, but went to the hospital that afternoon and they allowed me to see her for a few minutes. She was exhausted but assured me she would be all right. I left the hospital very troubled. It snowed that day and night and sister Russell and I walked down the mountain on a steep, narrow street to services. Somehow, I preached. When we climbed back up the mountain that night, the phone was ringing when we went into the house. It was her doctor at the hospital. I knew something was not right when he spoke to me. He said they had tried to induce natural labor and, that failing, they had tried forceps without success. He said, "We need to do a Caesarean section but under law cannot do it without your permission." Then he said something that nearly gave me heart failure. He said, "Mr. Adams, there in not much chance that the child will survive and we have to do this to save your wife." He told me he wanted me to come to the hospital as soon as I could. I told him to proceed with the C-section. It was still snowing heavily, but somehow I got that Opel down the mountain and to Kvinne Klinnekin. A nurse escorted me to a small area just outside the delivery room. I have never prayed any harder. I crossed a hundred bridges in my mind.

But in a little while I heard a baby cry. A nurse came through the door and gave me a big smile as she passed by hurriedly. Wilson Adams had made his entrance into the world on December 29, 1957. He was healthy. Bobbie was weak and traumatized when she came to and heard voices all around her speaking Norwegian. She had to remain in the hospital for two weeks. My debate started the next week after Wilson was born and the hospital and I had a stand-off about rules. They told me the only time I could come was between 7 and 9 each night. After the debate started, that meant I could not see her or the baby at all. When they became hardnosed about it, I told them I would be there in the afternoons to visit her and, if they tried to stop me, I would bring my attorney with a court order. I also told them what I thought of their lack of humanity. That is still part of my objection to socialized medicine. Well, they finally relented and the nurses even served us tea when I came. Bobbie's morale was at the lowest ebb I ever saw during the years we were married. When we finally got her and Wilson home, Mary Russell was a great blessing to us and I honestly don't know how we would have managed without her. At that point, there were no brothers or sisters in Christ to call.

The Debate

We had 25-30 to attend the debate. Not many you say? Well, there it seemed like a multitude. A. D. Norris was an eloquent speaker and came well prepared. He was a professor in a university in Yorkshire, England. He was the ablest man I have met in debate. He was also honest enough to accept the consequences of his argument. We debated about the establishment and nature of the kingdom. He had written that, in the millennium, "Christadelphian activities would be transferred from the arena of debate to that of military coercion." I read his statement to the audience and asked him if, in his next speech, he would tell us if he stood by that. He said he most certainly did. That did not set well with Norwegians who had been subservient to the Nazis just a little more than a decade before. The debate opened doors for more studies with new contacts.

Hope and Heartbreak

The first convert came in March, 1958, six months after we began. His name was Dag Bjornstad, a 22-year-old university student. From the time he attended the first meeting, this seriously minded young man studied with me two or three times a week at our house. He was a bright student and full of questions. One day he asked me, "If what you are teaching me is the truth, then I and my family and my countrymen are lost. Why have you waited so long to come and tell us?" That question haunted me then and even now. On a cold Sunday afternoon, I baptized him at an inlet from a fjord. A number of lakes were frozen. We changed clothes behind some rocks along the shore. I thought of the picture Arley Moore had showed me of his baptizing a man in freezing weather at Seward, Alaska. Dag began to help right away. Before long he was making talks. He expressed interest in preaching and we were able to raise some support for him. He was then single and did not require as much. He also still lived at home. We were never able to reach his family. I taught Dag everything

I knew to teach him. When we boarded our ship to begin the voyage home in September, 1959, Dag stood with five others who had obeyed the gospel, along with Mason and Louise Harris and Bill and Mary Lou Pierce (who had come to join us in the work by then), as they came to see us off. Through tears I said to Bobbie, "Dag will stand till the judgment."

But I was wrong. He left the faith and joined the Baptist church. He came to be influenced by an older preacher whom the institutional brethren in Oslo thought they had converted. I am partly responsible for what happened. I had opened the door for friendship and some cooperation with some who had gone from Texas to Oslo just before we went to Bergen. They had me for a meeting and I invited them to come to Bergen with the warning that, if they publicly advocated the sponsoring church or related practices, I would just as publicly oppose them. They all respected that. But when we had this "converted Baptist" preacher for a meeting (he stayed in our home), that is when he met Dag and formed more of a friendship with him than I knew at the time. We had some discussions in our home with this man and his wife, which led me to have some serious misgivings about him. When he defected, he led Dag with him. This was a serious blow to the work in Bergen.

But we had done what we came to do. We had made a start. After we had been there for a year, Mason and Louise Harris came. They lived in our house for a few months until they could locate their own place. We got along fine and leaned on each other in the work. The Harrises stayed five years in Norway and did much good work. Three months before we came home, Bill and Mary Lou Pierce came. They spent seven years in Norway, the last five of them trying to establish a work in Stavanger. Some others served for shorter periods in Bergen. The work almost died until Tom and Shirley Bunting came back. They spent eighteen years in that field. Their son Don and his wife, Cammie, spent some time in Stavanger. Their son, Terrell, and wife Karen worked a long time along with Tom and Shirley and then for several years after that. Terrell had partly grown up there and spoke the language without any trace of accent. At the present time their daughter Renee is married to Heath Robertson and they have just gone to Bergen to work with the church. The church is small. But they have an adequate meeting place which is well located. The work continues to be slow and hard. You will not read reports of many conversions as we see from India, the Philippines, or Central and South America. The liberal efforts in Norway, Sweden, and Denmark have all failed.

It has been my pleasure to return to the land of the midnight sun a number

Bilag til «Skandinavisk Kristen» nr. 2. Februar 1959.

Evangelist Connie W. Adams

KRISTI KIRKE i OSLO innbyr Dem herved på det hjerteligste til en rekke spesielle møter som tar sikte på å føre Dem nærmere til Gud.

Evangelist Connie W. Adams, Bergen vil tale over følgende emner:

Onsdag 18. feb.: «Den største historie om kjærlighet.»
Torsdag 19. » : «Kristi rike — nærværende eller i fremtiden — er det åndelig?»
Fredag 20. » : «Kristi kongedømmes tilblivelse.»
Lørdag 21. » : «Kan religiøs splittelse være velbehagelig for Gud?»
Søndag 22. » : «Nesten en kristen.»

Møtene holdes hver aften kl. 19.30 i FOLKETS HUS, SAL F.
Youngsgt. 13.

Meeting advertisement for Oslo, Norway (1958).

of times to conduct meetings and we plan another such effort in the summer of 2009 when we go to work with the Robertsons for five weeks.

To all who have in the past, or who continue at the present, to support the work in Norway, please remember Paul's admonition, "Be not weary in well doing, for in due season, we shall reap, if we faint not" (Gal. 6:9).

Chapter 7

Readjusting

Though we were only in Norway for two years, we came back to face many readjustments. Plans were made for us to locate in Newbern, Tennessee which was only forty miles from Fulton, Kentucky where Bobbie's parents lived. Our former classmate and good friend, Jere Frost, had been with the church at Newbern during a critical time. The preacher before him was institutional and tried to take that church along with him. They had built a nice brick building on Highway 51 which ran right through town. But the elders and most of the church took a firm stand and, in time the liberals left, bought the old property on Tyler St., where the church had met before erecting the new building on Main Street. Jere Frost came shortly after that and had to help settle things down. He did his work well. When he decided to move to Birmingham, Alabama, he gave the brethren my name and they contacted me about moving there to begin work in January, 1960. More about that later.

We returned in September, 1959 and, after a visit with my family in Virginia and Bobbie's folks in Kentucky, I conducted several meetings that fall and visited churches which had supported our work in Norway to give them a first hand report. I held meetings at Southeast in Akron, Ohio; Glenwood Hills, Decatur, Georgia; Hardies Chapel at Gordon, Georgia; Covington, Georgia; and West Avenue in San Antonio, Texas. But it had been two years since I had spoken to audiences of any size. While I had conducted meetings in Oslo, Norway; Gothenborg, Sweden; and Copenhagen, Aarhus, and Odense in Denmark, these were all small groups and over time you adjust your delivery to fit the size of the crowd. It took me a while to feel like I was really preaching again. In the first couple of meetings (and for a time after that), I would have the Norwegian word or phrase on the tip of my tongue and struggle to remember what to say in English. But the brethren were patient and encouraging. In San Antonio I worked with Robert Turner, a great man, excellent preacher, thinker, and writer.

Things had changed a lot in two years and more and more lines had been drawn among brethren, including where Robert Turner was working. They had a large building and a number had left over the institutional controversy.

He told me of a brother who came into his study all excited and wanted to know, "Brother Turner, are you anti?" Robert did not answer. So, he repeated the question, "Brother Turner, are you anti?" Robert said nothing. The brother became exasperated and said, "Don't you hear me, are you anti?" Robert calmly said, "Well, I was waiting for you to finish your sentence. Am I anti what?" That got to the heart of the problem. Some brethren thought that "anti" was something bad but they did not have a clue what they meant by it. All of us are surely against something, if we faithfully serve the Lord. Robert and Vivian Turner introduced me to Mexican food. It was a great improvement over the bland Norwegian diet. He said to me, "Now, if it does not make you sweat, you got cheated." I think of that every time I enjoy Mexican food.

One of the readjustments was the advancement of the division. With the exception of the Ohio Valley (and a few other places), in the west, southwest and south, the lines were tightly drawn by 1959 when we came home from Norway.

We had some financial adjustments to make. We came home with a child and the extra expense that involves. Also, we sold our furniture and were to move into an almost empty house. One of the elders at Newbern helped us get some appliances at discount and also some furniture, but even at discount, they had to be paid for. The church at Newbern agreed to provide us a very good house, right next to the meeting house, and to pay us $100 a week. In 1960, that was considered a good wage for a preacher. But we were on a very tight budget. We had brought an Opel station wagon home with us from Norway and it was economical to operate. Before going to Norway we had started a small investment in a mutual fund. We put $25 a month into it. I met with the elders and asked them if they would object to my selling mutual funds on the side, as long as it did not interfere with my work. They said they had no objection. So I became a salesman for Waddell and Reed out of Kansas City, Missouri. I spent a couple of nights a week at this and it helped to get our financial house in order. By the time we left Newbern, I phased out that work. Most of the members there did not even know of that work and I did not solicit business among them. I have always had a problem about preachers using their spiritual relationships to sell a product. One brother complained to me one time about a certain preacher, "I love him and love to hear him preach, but it seems like every time he comes, he has something he wants to sell me."

Main Street church building in Newbern, Tennessee (1960).

But there was another adjustment. I was a misfit at Newbern. That was not the fault of the brethren there; it was my fault. The work was laid back and slow paced. They were willing for me to do as much as I wanted to do, but I could not seem to stir up much enthusiasm. I suffered from guilt feelings about leaving the work in Bergen. Our bodies were in Newbern, Tennessee, but my heart, at least, was in Norway. We had a radio program on Sunday mornings. Franklin T. Puckett was preaching in Dyersburg, Tennessee, eight miles south, at the old Market Street congregation, which had helped support us in Norway. He was gone a lot in meetings and I ended up preaching on their five day a week program about as much as he did. Home studies were hard to come by. Religious roots and prejudices were deep seated in a town of 2,500 people. In two and a half years, we baptized seven, restored eight, and had five place membership. With an already established church of 160 people, we baptized seven. We had started from scratch in Norway where we did not know one soul and yet baptized six in two years. What was wrong? Was I expecting too much? At Glenwood Hills we baptized many people and had more home studies than we could keep up with. What I did not take into account was the fact that the church had suffered a division in a small town and everybody knew it. The church at Newbern has been faithful through the years and has done much good work. They helped us to get back on our feet and we have many good memories of our time there.

Roy E. Cogdill

Our second son, Martin, was born on March 3, 1961. He was delivered by the same doctor who delivered his mother and in the same hospital in Fulton, Kentucky. When he was a baby, he cried a lot at night. The doctor said the only thing wrong with him was that he was spoiled and we would have to tough it out and let him "cry it out." We were in the process of doing that when Roy E. Cogdill came to Newbern for a meeting. He stayed with us. One afternoon, we put Martin down for a nap about the time brother Cogdill tried to take one. Finally he came out of his room and said, "Aren't you going to get that poor little fellow? He's crying his eyes out?" Bobbie told him what the doctor had said. But brother Cogdill would not hear of it. He went in the bedroom, picked him up, and brought him out in the living room to a rocking chair where he softly cuddled him and rocked him for a long time. Of course, that is what Martin wanted in the first place, and it took a while to get him settled after the meeting. But that was a side of Roy Cogdill which some never saw. He loved little children and they loved him.

The bulletin at Newbern was called the *Newbern Admonisher* and we dealt with some of the unscriptural activities going on in western Tennessee among institutional brethren. We hit a few raw nerves and some of the teachers at Freed-Hardeman College took a few swings at us. G. K. Wallace wrote a sarcastic piece in the *Gospel Advocate* and referred to me as "Confused Connie." All of this finally led to a debate between Roy Cogdill and Guy N. Woods. Main Street in Newbern agreed to support brother Cogdill and another church in the county endorsed brother Woods. It fell my lot to correspond with both men to arrange the debate. There were twenty-four letters in the total correspondence. I wrote two letters to brother Cogdill and he wrote two to me. The remaining letters were between brother Woods and me. He haggled over every point and sought every advantage possible. Finally, he agreed to the same propositions they had debated in the fall of 1957 in Birmingham, which debate is in print. We wanted a date in the fall but brother Woods gave us an ultimatum. We would have it in December, the week right before Christmas, or not at all. It was to be a six night debate with three nights on the orphan home question and three on the Herald of Truth and the sponsoring church issue. Brother Cogdill had to get home to Oklahoma from meetings in California to be there in time and had to drive through an ice storm in the bargain. But he agreed in the very first letter to come whenever brother Woods would agree to it. I am fully convinced that the date insisted upon was because school would be out for the holidays and the students from Freed-Hardeman College would not be able to attend.

We had overflow crowds in the Main Street building for the debate. There was a balcony in the building and it was packed. Many preachers came from far and near. Franklin T. Puckett moderated for brother Cogdill and Alan E. Highers part of the time for brother Woods. W. L. Totty moderated for some of it. The debate essentially covered the same ground as the one in Birmingham and did much good in that local area.

After Martin was born, Bobbie had her hands full at services. I was either teaching a class or in the pulpit and could not help manage the children. To keep Wilson from taking advantage of the situation, we told him that if his mother had to take him out and spank him during the service, he would get another one from me when we got home. One Sunday, I saw her take him out and spank him. Someone else had to hold Martin while she attended to that chore. Wilson would linger after services and walk to the house with me. On the way, I said, "Wilson, didn't your mother have to take you out this morning?" He said, "Uh huh." I said, "Did she spank you?" He said, "Uh huh." "Well," I said, "don't we have a rule about that?" Again, "Uh huh." He was not volunteering anything. I asked him, "How does that go?" He said, "If Momma spanks me at church; you spank me when we get home." I said, "I thought that is the way that works. When we get home, you know what we have to do, don't you?" He sighed and said, "Uh huh." Then I asked him if he would rather have his spanking before dinner or after. He said, "Before." So when we got in the house I got the little plywood paddle which we kept on top of the refrigerator (and called the Board of Education), and took the little four-year-old by the hand. Just as we closed the door into the bedroom, he looked up at me and said, "Now, Daddy, let's be reasonable about this." What do you do with such a child?

The Spring Creek Trial

While we were at Newbern, the church at Spring Creek (about fifteen miles northeast of Jackson, Tennessee) suffered a tragic division. An effort was made to hastily appoint elders who were sympathetic with the institutional position and to screen out preachers like L. E. Sloan, Earl Fly, Grover Stevens, and others who had been instrumental in beginning that work and who had preached in many meetings there and baptized most of the members. At the time, W. A. Bradfield from Freed-Hardeman College was preaching for them on Sundays.

They had a business meeting at which it was announced that they were going to appoint elders that night in that very meeting. They were going to do it by majority vote. Several men were present who did not normally come to such meetings and who were not faithful in attending services. Some of the brethren objected and suggested that it would be good to have some sermons on the subject and then put forth names and give the congregation time to make objections if they had any. But those controlling the meeting insisted that they were going to put forth names that night and that all objections should be made then and there. Four names were put forth. J.C. Fincher made objections to all of them and some others agreed. Then the chairman said they had heard the objections and it was time to vote. Some of the men refused to take part in that since they thought this was not the right way to go about this important decision. When the vote was counted, there were eight who voted for the proposed elders and six who voted against them. Of the eight, four of them were the men themselves whose names were under consideration. Had they not voted for themselves, they would have lost the election six to four. The meeting turned ugly. Those who objected to what was done decided to meet in the afternoons at a different time. Those who favored the new elders changed the lock. The others cut off the new lock and used the building anyhow. The new elders sought an injunction from the court forbidding the use of the building to those who had opposed their "election."

It got in the newspapers. Finally there was a four day hearing in Jackson. Both sides called "expert" witnesses. The objectors did not instigate the suit. They were required by the court to appear. Each side engaged an attorney. The woman who represented the elders and those who stood with them, called G. K. Wallace, H. A. Dixon (president of Freed-Hardeman College), and W. A. Bradfield. All of these men were connected to the college at Henderson. The gist of their testimony was to the effect that in a church without elders, business is conducted by the will of the majority of the male members and that what was done was perfectly right. L. E. Sloan, Earl Fly, and Franklin T. Puckett all testified that there are divine principles set forth in the Scriptures which should govern the conduct of the Lord's people and that the church is not a democracy. The judge ruled in favor of the majority. It was close since there were fifty-one who stood with the elected elders and forty-nine who opposed. The forty-nine had to get out and start over. They did just that, and have grown while the other group has diminished.

In the testimony of W. A. Bradfield, he was asked if a majority agreed to put eight names in a hat, have someone draw out four names, and by mutual agreement, these first four names would be the elders, would that be all right? Brother Bradfield did not want to answer. The judge directed him to answer the question. Finally, he said, "Yes, if that is what the majority decided."

As sad and tragic as that was, there was one incident which relieved the tension. When J. C. Fincher was being questioned, he was asked if it was true that he refused to bow his head and participate in the closing prayer at the end of that business meeting. He said, "Yes Mam, that is true." She wondered why a Christian would refuse to participate in a prayer. The judge interrupted and asked for an explanation. Brother Fincher said that they all had acted shamefully and that prayer at that point was a farce and didn't get any higher than the ceiling. He said, "If the Lord was in that meeting, He left when we got started." Even the judge shook his head and laughed. I witnessed that whole hearing and hope never to see such a sad spectacle again. Politics and power plays have no place in the church.

A Great Blessing

One of the great blessings of our time at Newbern was the association we had with Frank and Evelyn Puckett. Several times, I would need help with a passage and would call him to assist me. He never turned me down, though he was always very busy. Brother Puckett was a self-made Bible scholar. In his early years of preaching, he had memorized large portions of Scripture while plowing on a farm near Calico Rock, Arkansas. He would read a paragraph at the end of the row and then recite it as he followed the plow back down the field. He took courses in Hebrew and Greek and other subjects which helped to develop him into one of the great preachers of his generation. He could hold an audience in rapt attention for an hour and a half or more. I heard him quote several chapters without opening his Bible during the course of a sermon. This was not done as a show. Many of the older preachers could do that. He told me once of what some of the preachers used to do to not only pass the time, but to sharpen each other. They would sit in a circle and one would quote a verse. The man next to him would have to quote either the next verse or the one before it. He said sometimes they would go around a circle of several men a number of times before one would be stumped and have to drop out.

Franklin T. Puckett

When I would call him and ask if he could find some time to help me with a passage, he would say, "Come on down." I would drive the eight miles to Dyersburg and he would take me to an upstairs room where he had two large, cane bottomed rocking chairs (similar to those you see on the front porch at Cracker Barrel Restaurants). He had caned them himself, as that was a hobby he enjoyed. I would tell him what my problem was and he would start. Sometimes it would take two hours, sometimes longer, but it was always rich. I had met him while a student in Florida when he came for lectures and had also had some contact with him because of mutual interest in the work in Atlanta. He had preached a number of years at West End in that city. Brother Puckett was one of the most dignified men, in his carriage, I have ever known. He was always well dressed, stood erect, and resembled what you would think a Supreme Court Justice would look like. But one thing did not fit that image. He played the fiddle, and played it well. One day he called me and said, "Can Evelyn and I come up to Newbern? I need a break and need to play my fiddle." They came and I got out my guitar and while Bobbie and Evelyn made spaghetti, we played some Arkansas hoedown music. At one point I got tickled. He stopped and said, "What are you laughing about?" I said, "This is the most unlikely sight in the world. Here you are dressed up like a judge and sawing on that fiddle." He grinned and said, "Aw, play!" Acquaintance with such men is among my richest memories. Someone wrote that "we are a part of all we have met." When I think of such men, I earnestly hope that is true.

Chapter 8

From Gatorland to Buckeye Country

During the lectures at Florida College in 1962, a short in the electrical system on our 1957 Oldsmobile burned out all the wiring. That meant I would have to stay a few days longer than planned to get it repaired. James P. Miller knew a good mechanic who agreed to repair the damage and loaned me a car to drive while I waited. Brother Miller also told me that the Pine Hills church in Orlando was looking for a preacher and put me in touch with Jerry Belchick who had been preaching for them while teaching school. Arrangements were made for me to spend the weekend there and preach for that growing church in what was then a growing community. The church numbered 175-180, had a good building, and provided a house for the preacher. They had no elders but there was obviously great potential for growth. I met with the brethren on Sunday night and we took turns questioning each other about a number of things. They offered me the work and I told them I would need a little time to think about it and discuss it with my wife when I got back to Newbern. The decision was made and in June, 1962 we moved back to Florida.

Orlando then was a city of about 100,000. That was before Disney came to town. It was then a quiet city away from the tourist attractions. There were four good congregations in the city: Pine Hills, Holden Heights (now South Bumby), Azalea Park, and Par Street (which has now disbanded). James P. Miller had preached at the Jefferson Street church and had significant influence in that area. Holden Heights began as a peaceful "swarm" from Jefferson Street and quickly grew. Jerry Belchick, a former classmate at Florida Christian College who graduated with me in 1953, was the preacher. The institutional issue raised its ugly head in Orlando resulting in Jefferson Street going institutional while Holden Heights held the line. Tensions were high, as they were in other parts of the country. While brother Miller was in Orlando, he had a debate with Morris B. Book of the Christian Church on instrumental music in worship. That debate was well attended and was put in print. In just a few years, the church at Holden Heights grew significantly. Many of the members lived in the Pine Hills area, on the west side of town and it was decided that a congregation should be started in that growing area with Holden Heights supporting and encouraging the new work. Jerry Belchick went along to preach for the new congregation. He began teaching high school to supplement his income.

From the very first, the work was pleasant. We had a few internal problems but there was a good spirit among the brethren and we were able to handle them peacefully. The work continued to grow. We baptized a good number of people. In addition to that, we had a number of families to move into the area from other parts of the country. Some of these came out of liberal backgrounds and we had many studies with some of them. Some were so prejudiced that they did not want to be associated with an "anti" church. But some were open minded and, once they really studied the issues involved, became faithful and active members at Pine Hills.

In 1964, I had a debate with O. G. Lodge of the Church of God. He called me and challenged for a debate. We had bought space in the *Orlando Sentinel* newspaper to oppose the healing campaign of the faith healer, Leroy Jenkins. Lodge took exception to some things I had written in those articles. We met and agreed to a four night debate with two nights on salvation by faith, before and without water baptism, and two nights on the identity of the church. We advertised it in the newspaper and in *Searching The Scriptures*. Careful preparation was made and our building was to be the venue. The first night, we had an overflow crowd. But then a strange thing happened. The next morning Mr. Lodge called me to say that his "bishop" had forbidden him to continue the debate. This gentleman had come to Pine Hills the night before but would not come in the building. He listened through a side door. One of the brethren patrolled the parking lot and spotted him in the shadows by the door. He invited him to come inside, but he refused. He told Lodge that he did not get permission from his superiors for this debate and that, if he continued, there would be a price to pay. The "price" was that Mr. Lodge was 62 years old and three years away from being able to retire with a pension. If he did not obey his "bishop" he would lose his retirement. He was very apologetic and said he knew it put us in a predicament. People were coming from far and near for the Tuesday night session and we could not stop them. Earl Fly, from Holden Heights, was my moderator and he suggested that I go ahead on Tuesday night and present a summary of the material I had prepared for the last two nights. I talked with as many brethren at Pine Hills as I could reach that day and they thought that would be the best thing to do.

That night, another overflow crowd gathered. Earl Fly explained what had happened. Mr. Lodge and his wife were present and listened attentively to my presentation. I had prepared a large cloth chart on "The New Testament Church" and just preached through that material. At the end of the meeting, I asked Mr. Lodge if he would like to say something. He arose and said that Earl Fly had correctly explained what had happened. He was very apologetic but told the audience that the matter was out of his hands and that he had to obey orders or else. Then he commended my speech and said, "Maybe it is just as well we did not have the last two nights as we had planned, because I could not answer what Mr. Adams said."

There was a spirit of comaraderie among the preachers in the area as well as among the brethren in general. Jim Ward, who replaced Earl Fly, Jerry Belchick, Tom O'Neal, and Marshall E. Patton were all congenial co-workers. The Cuban missile crisis took place early in our stay in Orlando. For days we heard the drone of planes flying military supplies and equipment to the southern part of Florida. My mother was so concerned that she called and suggested that we come to Virginia until the crisis was over. I told her I felt safer in Florida than I would in Virginia, just 120 miles from Washington, D.C.

There were some "pickers" in the number at Pine Hills. I met a man in the waiting room at one of the hospitals, whose wife was a faithful member at Pine Hills. He was a wayward Christian and having a battle with drinking. But he was also a very good musician. He tuned pianos for a living. He had made a seven-string steel guitar which required special tuning and had written several Hawaiian guitar songs, one of which had been used in a movie based in Hawaii. Lynn Robinson, Bob West, Frank Belue, and I decided we would spend some time with Bernard Denoe and see if we could help him overcome his drinking problem. That resulted in his being restored and becoming very active in the work of the church. We also put together a band dubbed "The Sons of the Palmettos." We played for social get-togethers, and did a couple of shows in Orlando and Jacksonville to raise funds for Florida College. We were also invited to perform at a rodeo at Clay Sink, near Dade City. That was more than interesting. The platform they built, on which we were to perform, was above the bull

Adams Family (1962).

pen. Right under us was a large Brahma bull. He was big and mean. During one of our numbers, Bernard hit some hot licks on his steel guitar and that bull just about came unraveled. We all thought he would tear down that pen, platform and all, and that we would all be riding the bull before it was over.

Those three years were rewarding in the work of the Pine Hills church and in the many friendships we formed. There were times the last year at Pine Hills when we had over 300 in attendance (I believe 313 was the record) and had to open the sliding doors into two classrooms on the side to seat the crowd. Sadly, the Pine Hills community has become a high crime area and the church has diminished in size to a small number. Some internal problems contributed to that decline, before the deterioration of the community.

The Akron Years

In February, 1965, I returned to Norway for a month of preaching. I held meetings in Bergen and Stavanger where there were small congregations, but also in several other cities on the west coast of Norway in an attempt to reach people from those places who had written for tracts or Bible correspondence courses. Just before I left, Cecil Willis called me from Akron, Ohio to say that the Brown Street church where he was working wanted to engage a second preacher to work with him, to be available for meetings wherever a door opened and to publish a monthly bulletin to circulate as widely as possible in that part of the country. Ohio Valley was the last part of the country to firmly divide over the sponsoring church, church support of institutions, and related issues. Many churches were on the fence. It was a critical time and it appeared to me that much good could be done in encouraging those who wanted to stand for the truth and in educating those who were undecided. We were happy in Orlando, the work was progressing toward being able to appoint elders, but somehow I was interested in the challenge. After I arrived in Norway, Bobbie wrote and said the elders at Brown Street really wanted to talk to me and proposed that I fly to Akron before returning to Orlando, so that, if I was not interested, the brethren at Pine Hills would not need to be upset. I still have the letters Bobbie wrote me during that time. She was willing to go wherever I thought I could do the most good. She was contented in Orlando, the children were happy there, but she also sensed the urgency of that work in Ohio. I decided to at least go to Akron and talk to them about it before returning to Orlando. One of the elders met me in Cleveland. We had a couple of productive meetings and I spent a day with Cecil Willis during which we discussed the pros and cons of two preachers working together.

Cecil Willis and I had been classmates at Florida Christian College and graduated together in the spring of 1953. We were already good friends, but both of us knew that there were potential problems with two men working together in the same church. If I accepted the offer, we would divide our time between the local work and gospel meetings. While one of us was in a meeting, the other would be at Brown Street. We would have to coordinate our plans so as to keep each other informed as to what we had preached on or how far we had progressed in a Bible class. We even discussed how we would handle things if some members tried to array one preacher against the other. The elders offered a good salary for that time and housing allowance since we would have to buy a house. They also agreed to cover travel expenses and any shortfall in support should the meeting income not be enough to provide that. I told them I was very interested but that I would need a little time to talk it over with Bobbie. We set a time to give them my answer and I headed back to Orlando with mixed emotions.

Bobbie was supportive every step of the way. We decided to go and give it our best. The brethren at Pine Hills were disappointed, but understanding. One good brother (who later was appointed an elder) said, "If you want to go up to

Brown Street church building (1965)

the land of snow and ice, you go ahead, but you are not taking Bobbie and those little boys. You can just leave them here where it is warm." The wife of one of the elders at Brown Street was a real estate agent. She sent us information about schools, houses for sale, and a number of things about the Akron area in general. We flew to Akron so Bobbie could meet the brethren and in one week we were able to buy a house just a few blocks from the meeting house. It was amazing that we were able to do all of that, with the paper work, in such a short time.

We moved to Akron in June, 1965, to begin what I consider one of the most fruitful and interesting periods of life. The attendance at Brown Street was usually in the range of 325-350. The church met in a renovated hanger in what was known as Firestone Park (named for the tire company). Akron was then a city of about 300,000 and was the tire capitol of the world. Such companies as Firestone, Goodyear, B. F. Goodrich, Sieberling, Mohawk, Dunlop, and some others had plants and headquarters there. The work force was made up of Buckeyes (natives of Ohio) but also those who had migrated north from West Virginia, Kentucky, Tennessee, Alabama, and a few other southern states. It was a smelly city, but wages were good and life was pleasant for us.

The church had built a very nice classroom addition. Not only did Cecil Willis and I have adequate office space, but there was one large classroom which became the scene of special winter classes. We had a number of men who wanted to preach, or else enhance their abilities in that direction. Also, there were some younger men in the Akron area from other congregations who wanted to study with us. The first year, we planned a class on Bible Geography and History. Such young men as Robert Archer, Bruce Taylor, Jerry Parks, Larry DeVore, and a number of others came with big notebooks and were obviously ready to make the most of it. These classes were conducted during the winter months. Since Cecil and I alternated being away in meetings, we each taught segments of these classes. After Cecil moved to Marion, Indiana, Ferrell Jenkins came to work with us for a couple of years and we expanded these classes to include weekday classes, as well. We taught Sermon Preparation and Delivery, How to Study the Bible, the Minor Prophets, Church History, Personal Evangelism, and several other subjects.

During those years we averaged holding forty meetings with the number about equally divided between the two of us. We held many meetings for small, struggling churches. In one year, I preached in a courthouse, two store fronts, a small house with partitions removed to make space to seat about forty, in an American Legion hall, and a facility owned by the Daughters of the American Revolution. There were meetings with churches which were on the fence and some that were blissfully unaware that there even was an issue. One year they would have an institutional preacher, then the next, one who was non-institutional and then one who did not know what he believed. In the meantime, papers such as the *Bible Herald* were tilting toward more liberal views and practices and Ohio Valley College was clearly moving in that direction. Their annual lecture program reflected this as they invited well known men who were in the forefront of leading churches in the south and southwest away from the old paths. There were brethren who said they agreed with us in principle but did not like "how" we taught on the subject. In fact, some did not want us to preach on these issues at all. We often had brethren who would call us aside, soon after arrival, and say, "Now, we don't have any problem here about the Herald of Truth, or orphans homes, and we would just as soon that you did not mention these issues." I had a stock answer every time that happened. I would say, "Well, I thought I would preach one night on 'Why We Don't Use Instrumental Music.' Would that be all right?" They would always say, "Oh yes, that would be fine." Then I would ask, "Are you having trouble here over that?" "Oh no" they would always answer. Then I would ask, "Why is it all right for me to preach on instrumental music when you are not having a problem with it here, but wrong for me to preach on things which concern the nature, organization, and work of the church, when you say you are not having a problem here about any of that?" They never had a sensible answer. Both Cecil and I (and other good men in that area) did preach on it.

One such incident was at Wellsburg, West Virginia. W. O. (Barney) Winland was preaching for them and he took a stand on these issues and persuaded the brethren to have me for a meeting. One of the elders was pretty well informed, but the others were not. The night before I arrived, the elders attended a meeting in Weirton where a former preacher from Wellsburg was preaching. He called them aside and scared them half to death about me. He wondered why they would have such a "church divider" and "hobby rider" and a few other choice descriptions. These men went to Barney's house before going home and one of them said, "If Adams even mentions the Herald of Truth or orphan homes, I am going to stand right up and stop him." When I arrived the next day, I could tell Barney was worried. Finally, he told me what had happened and asked me what I planned to do. I told him I was going to preach the truth the best I could and, if I preached something that was not true, I would expect an elder to oppose it. The first night I preached on "What Is Truth?" In the process I discussed the value and the demands of truth. This one elder sat leaning forward with one hand on the back of the pew in front of him as if he were ready to spring up at any time. The second night I spoke of "Bible Authority" (how it is expressed and applied). By the end of that sermon, the anxious elder relaxed a little and leaned back into a more comfortable position. The third night my subject was the "Organization and Work of the Church." On Sunday, the day the meeting ended, we had a special afternoon service at which I spoke on "What Is Wrong with the Herald of Truth?" We advertised that there would be a question period at the end of the sermon. We had the house full. There were two board members of Ohio Valley College present, and several liberal-leaning preachers, plus some who were far beyond the leaning stage. We had very few questions. But when the service was over and the crowd thinned out, the elders came to me in a group (there were four) and the brother who was ready to stand up and stop me, served as spokesman for them. He said they owed me an apology and thanked me for having the courage to preach what they needed to hear, and that they were convinced that I had taught the truth and had sounded needed warnings. They asked if I could come back for a longer meeting and I agreed to do so. Then they led me to the bulletin board where they had a sheet listing future meetings with the speakers. They said they were going to cancel every liberal on the schedule and asked me to recommend some good, sound men they could invite. I named several and some of them were invited. After Barney Winland left the work, they hired my brother-in-law, Thomas Icard, who was the first preacher to live in the new house they had built for a preacher.

During those years, there were preachers who preached on the principles but did not make specific applications. The churches where they worked ended up institutional. Cecil Willis expressed it well. He said, "When you draw a picture of a pig on the chalk board, you need to write under it, in big letters PIG, so everyone will get the point."

The Enlightener

I edited a monthly bulletin called *The Enlightener*, which we began as a means of teaching brethren in that area on the issues which were leading brethren astray. Cecil Willis edited *Truth Magazine* which had a special effect in the Ohio Valley, as well as nationally. James P. Needham, William Wallace, and Earl Robertson were associate editors and I was asked to serve in that capacity, as well. But *The Enlightener* was a four page, neatly printed bulletin format with a local flavor and which was published as a part of the work at Brown Street. Many brethren sent lists of names to be added to the list. By the time I left Brown Street, we were mailing 9,000 of these each issue. The heaviest circulation was in Ohio, West Virginia, Indiana, Illinois, and Michigan. Institutional preachers sometimes would take a copy of it into the pulpit, hold it up and tell the audience that this was trash and that, if they received it in the mail, they should throw it out with the other trash. That served to whet the curiosity of many who started reading it and decided it made sense. The material was written by Cecil and me. That bulletin opened many doors for gospel meetings and led to a number of people taking a stand for the truth. During those five years, there were twenty-five congregations in the Ohio Valley which took a firm stand for the truth and I know that *The Enlightener* played a part in that taking place.

Some complained that we were interfering with the autonomy of other churches by sending this bulletin to them. Some attempts were made to shame us into removing the names of every member from certain churches. Our practice was to remove any name from the mailing list upon a simple request from the recipient to do so. But we did not allow another party to censor the private mail of anyone. If someone wrote and asked us to remove his name and made some comment beyond a request for removal, we always wrote to him to discuss the point of the comment. This resulted in many correspondences, some of which led to people seeing and accepting the truth. We met people all over the Ohio Valley who thanked us for the bulletin and for helping to open their eyes. When Ferrell Jenkins came to work with us, he shared the writing.

The Enlightener had a major part in three debates taking place. Cecil Willis met Clifton Inman in debates in Parkersburg, West Virginia and Dayton, Ohio and Ferrell Jenkins debated Bill Heinselman in Akron, Ohio. All three of these debates did much good. *The Willis-Inman Debate* in Parkersburg is still in print. One of the unique things about that debate is the thorough exposure of the argument that the Herald of Truth was simply an expedient. That argument was not only exposed but demolished. In the Jenkins-Heiselman debate, there were two very able men involved. Bill Heinselman was a very animated speaker (in contrast to Clifton Inman, who tended to be pretty dry). But Heinselman was also given to sarcasm. One night he said he was "catching it from both sides." The elders where he preached had told him, so he said, that he was letting Ferrell Jenkins "out-nice" him. Ferrell not only pressed his points with clarity and simplicity, but he had a big toothy grin most of the time, whereas Bill Heinselman was cutting and sarcastic at times. That was one of the better debates, in terms of arguments presented and answered, and I wish it had been put into print.

Bobbie and Francis Birdwell (whose husband, O. C., preached at Barberton), handled the mailing list for the bulletin and worked together addressing and preparing it for mailing. When the Jenkins came to Brown Street, Bobbie and Elizabeth Jenkins did that work. They developed a special friendship. Ferrell and I were seldom home at the same time. Elizabeth and Bobbie would greet visitors and sometimes, as they brought the visitor to meet either Ferrell or my self, Elizabeth would raise a few eyebrows when she would say, "And this is *our* husband."

We had many good meetings at Brown Street with such men as James P. Needham, Roy Cogdill, James W. Adams, Luther Blackmon, James R. Cope, and others. Once when brother Cope was there, I sat down beside him on the front row before the meeting began and he was looking over his outline. It was scrawled onto a jagged piece of a brown paper bag. I said, "Brother Cope, it does look like the president of a college could have a more dignified looking outline than that." He said, "Aw, there's nothing wrong with it. It works fine." He was a joy to entertain. He was perfectly relaxed and made you feel that way. Someone said, "Jim Cope does not sit in a chair, he wears it." Our boys were delighted when he would shoot basketball with them. There was a special bond between the preachers in Akron during those years. They included Paul Casebolt, Weldon Warnock, Cecil Willis, Ferrell Jenkins, Austin Mobley, Truman Smith, O. C. Birdwell, Morris Norman, Luther Blackmon, E. A. Dicus and George Lemasters. We were all on the same page and working shoulder to shoulder in the Lord's cause. We not only worked together in meetings, but we spent time together socially.

One of the great blessings of my life was the opportunity during the Akron years to become friends with Luther Blackmon. He nicknamed me "Connery" for some reason. He was a lover of country music and had an 8x10 autographed picture of Kitty Wells in his dining room. He planned several hoedown sessions at his house in Bedford, Ohio and would join in with the fun. He was a pretty good singer in his own right. I had met and heard him preach during college days and when I had preached at Cortez, he came for some meetings at West Braden-

Luther Blackmon

ton. That man could really preach. His memory was phenomenal, not only in being able to quote Scripture, but also facts of history, science, bits of literature and poetry, things which he said would "spice up a sermon." At Bedford, a suburb of Cleveland, he was in his later years and his health began to decline while he was there. I have tapes of six of his sermons preached at Bedford. On a trip to the northwest for some meetings, we listened to them and I told my wife that Luther could teach you more incidentally than some preachers could on purpose. His work in East Texas was legendary and often when preachers get together, some of the older ones enjoy telling stories about Luther Blackmon. He and Roy Cogdill had worked together at Norhill in Houston, where they divided their time in meetings and the local work. Later he did outstanding work at Red Bluff in Pasadena, Texas. He had a number of down home sayings which some called "Lutherisms." He said that he was raised two wagon greasings from town, so far out that you had to go toward town to hunt. Or he would describe someone as being "friendly as a wet dog." In his last years, he lost his memory. But he never lost his sense of humor or his taste in clothes. He was always well put together. He had a keen sense of what looked good on him. The last place he tried to do local work was at Berea, Ohio. During that time, I preached in a meeting at North Ridgeville, just west of Cleveland, and there was a Sunday afternoon singing. Luther came and they asked him to lead a song. He said before he began that he always loved to sing and was a fairly good song leader when he was younger. But he said since he had gotten older his brother told him that, when he sang, it "sounded like somebody strangling a cat with a newspaper." But aside from all the stories people remember about him, he was one capable preacher whose life touched the hearts of many people and got them started toward Heaven.

Cecil Willis

The Influence of Cecil Willis

The eight years Cecil Willis lived in Akron, Ohio were critical ones in the history of the church in that part of the country. Any fair historical assessment would have to conclude that his writing and preaching during those years had a profound effect on the Lord's work in the Ohio Valley. Any historian who ignores that influence has not done his homework. When *Truth Magazine* was about to fail and go out of business, he took on the task of editing it and developing it into a powerful force to defend and advance the old paths, not only in the Ohio Valley but throughout the country as well as in many other countries. He was an excellent student of the Bible and related subjects. His pen was powerful. He was diligent and tireless in his work habits. He continually prepared new material for his preaching and classes. When we moved to Brown Street, Cecil had already been there for six years. Hiram Crabtree, one of the elders then at Brown Street, paid him a high compliment. He said that after six years, his preaching "was as fresh as when he first came there." Some thought Cecil was aloof at times, and he might well have been. But I think it would be fairer to say that he was preoccupied. His mind was never far removed from the work of the Lord and his involvement in it. He was generous to a fault with what he owned. He was a master at delegating work. He could enlist your help in such a way as to make you think you were greatly blessed to have the opportunity to do what he asked you to do.

While James P. Needham was in a meeting at Brown Street, Stephen, one of Cecil's sons, had what was diagnosed as an epileptic seizure. This led to the decision to leave Brown Street and move to Marion, Indiana so he could be home more with his family until they were sure they had Steve's situation under control. He thought the two preacher arrangement at Brown Street was doing too much good for it not to continue, and urged the elders to find a man to replace him in that work. When he came and told me he would be moving and the reasons for it, we both wept, the first time I ever recall such an emotion from him.

While the family lived at Marion, Cecil's health deteriorated. He was taking a great amount of medication. I do not believe that his writing and his judgment about editorial decisions for the paper were as clear and sharp as they were earlier. In 1975, we made a trip together to the Philippines. The night we spent in Honolulu on our way there, he put together four future issues of the paper, while I watched a basketball game. After we arrived in the Philippines, he had a great deal of trouble with the heat. His blood pressure was elevated at times. While we were in Mindanao, at a town called Kidapawan where we were preaching in a school building, he finished his sermon on Ecclesiastes and went outside to cool off while I preached. About midway through my sermon, one of the brethren came running in, interrupted me, and said, "Come quick, something is wrong with brother Willis." I hurried outside where brethren had him stretched out on the ground. I ran to him and lifted up his head and asked what he thought was wrong. He said, "I think maybe I've had a stroke." Later diagnosis confirmed that to be the case. None of the brethren owned a vehicle. One of them flagged down a man on the road who had a station wagon. We loaded him in the back of that vehicle and two of the brethren went with us to Makilala, about twenty miles away where there was a small hospital. After they got his blood pressure down, I went back to Kidapawan, gathered our things and rented a van to take us and four brethren to Davao City so we could catch a plane back to Manila. We both agreed that he should remain in Manila and do what he could to teach those who could come to him while I went ahead to the places we had scheduled on the islands of Palawan and Romblon.

After returning from the Philippines, marriage problems reached a critical stage and he left for Texas and began a ten year period of his life which was a great waste. He divorced his wife, unscripturally, and married a younger woman in Texas. Many of his old friends and especially his brothers tried to talk with him but he closed the door to all such efforts. After the second marriage ended, he became more reflective and open to talking with some of us. During a meeting in Houston, I called him and told him we would be coming through Groveton the next day and that I would like to see him and talk with him about his soul. To my surprise, he said he would welcome that. He was then living with his parents at Woodlake, Texas and had been working as a security guard at the state penitentiary at Huntsville, Texas. My wife visited with his parents in the house while he and I sat for several hours on the back of a farm wagon out in the yard and talked. He admitted to me that he did not have a scriptural right to divorce his first wife and that his second marriage was wrong. He asked what he ought to do to make things right. The church at Conroe, Texas had withdrawn from him and I suggested that the place to start was with a letter expressing repentance to them. He went before the church at Groveton, where he had grown up and began preaching, read a statement of repentance, forwarded a copy of it to the church at Conroe, Texas; Marion, Indiana; and Brown Street in Akron to let those who had been so affected by his choices know he was trying to do what he could to make correction for his wrongs. I printed it in *Searching The Scriptures*. For the rest of his life, he took a low profile and was grateful for every opportunity he had to preach again. He worked with a small church in Fairbanks, Alaska for a while. He last worked with the church at Salem, Ohio. He died there from a heart attack. A number of others had a part in his restoration. I attended his funeral which was conducted at Brown Street and participated along with his brothers, Lewis and Mike. We spoke of his life and work, including the ten wasted years. "Let him that thinketh he standeth, take heed lest he fall" (1 Cor. 10:12). Many owe him a debt of gratitude for his faithful years of service. I do especially. In my lifetime, I know of nobody who wielded a greater influence in the Ohio Valley than Cecil Willis.

Summary of Five Good Years

During the time in Akron, with the two-preacher arrangement, we averaged forty gospel meetings a year. In spite of having to deal with controversial subjects, some of which involved tension, we baptized an average of 120 each of those years. That included the meetings and the work at Brown Street. Both Cecil Willis and Ferrell Jenkins were congenial co-workers and we had no trouble working together. One problem we had was that, while we could trade back and forth in the pulpit and Bible classes, the one thing we could not trade was the rapport we had with people in personal Bible studies. Each teacher has to build a bridge to his prospect and he can't trade that back and forth every other week. It led me to a one shot approach which has worked well there and elsewhere. After Ferrell Jenkins left, the elders decided to stop the two-preacher efforts and revert to a single preacher. I worked in that arrangement for a year with a greatly reduced meeting schedule. While we were there, Wilson obeyed the gospel. Bobbie completed her degree in Business Education at Akron University and did her practice teaching at Garfield High School. But Louisville, Kentucky came calling and we decided to answer that call and move to the Bluegrass state.

As special as these years were, it is the source of much sadness that more recently the elders at Brown Street have taken such a stand against those connected with *Truth Magazine*, and especially regarding the lecture program, that they have made it a test of fellowship and have cancelled meetings and cut off financial support from any brother who has spoken on this program. Cecil Willis was editor of the paper while he preached there, I was associate editor during my five years there, and Ferrell Jenkins wrote for the paper during those years. Weldon Warnock preached there for five years and served on the Guardian of Truth Foundation's Board during that time. Lewis Willis preached there for approximately twenty-five years and wrote for the paper during that time. The same could be said of many of the men who held meetings there. All of us spoke several times at the Florida College lectures during those years without one word of objection. Yet none of us would be welcome to preach there now. My story would not be fairly told without expressing the deep sorrow this has occasioned.

Chapter 9

Moving to Bluegrass Country

Kentucky had long held special interest for me. Bobbie was from Fulton, in the southwest corner of the state. While Kentucky had a reputation for fast horses, burley tobacco, and bourbon whiskey, there were many things about it which appealed to me. Bill Monroe, the father of bluegrass music was from Rosine, Kentucky. I had been an ardent fan of Kentucky basketball since 1950 when I saw Kentucky play Florida in Tampa. They had two all-Americans on that team, Cliff Hagan and Frank Ramsey. I had played basketball in high school and at Florida Christian College (we did not compete then with other schools but played in an industrial league), and thought I knew what basketball was all about. But after watching those Wildcats play, I turned to Bobbie and said, "You know, I don't think I have ever seen a real basketball game before now." I was hooked and followed the fortunes (and misfortunes) of the team ever since. Even in Norway, we heard some of the games on the Armed Forces Network. I take it personally when the "Cats" lose and when they win, I want them to win by a wide margin so it stings a little for the loser. Yes, Kentucky had several appeals. But the one that counted most was the opportunity to live and preach the gospel in this storied place.

No place on earth is more beautiful than Kentucky in the spring when the rolling hills of central Kentucky (the heart of the bluegrass country) come alive with redbud trees, dogwoods, azaleas, and a rainbow of colors in the blooming flowers. To drive through the horse farm country in the spring and see all that amid the endless stretches of white (or black) fences surrounding green, rolling pastures on which horses gently graze is good for what ails any man. I have often said to myself, or to Bobbie, "When the Lord made Kentucky, I know he smiled." Kentucky is really three distinct regions. Western Kentucky is fairly flat and runs from the delta near the convergence of the Mississippi and Ohio Rivers east to Bowling Green. The triangle from Louisville southwest toward Bowling Green and east toward Lexington is the heart of the real bluegrass country. From Lexington eastward is the mountain region. That is a world all its own. While much strip mining of coal had taken place in western Kentucky, eastern Kentucky has built its economy on mostly underground coal mining. The mountains are populated with the descendants of Scotch and Irish emigrants. The music which echoes through the hills and hollows ("hollers," if you are from those parts), finds its roots in Celtic music. The people generally tend to view you with a certain suspicion until you have proved yourself to be genuine. Then you have made friends for life. We have come to love the people we have met there and always enjoy opportunities to preach among them. I have taken the time and space to say all of this because we have met many people in other parts of the country who know nothing about the Commonwealth of Kentucky. Some, otherwise well educated people, have asked, "Now, let's see, what states border Kentucky?" So, in the interest of education, here is the answer. To our south is the state of Tennessee. To the east is Virginia and West Virginia. To the north lies Ohio, Indiana, and Illinois and to the west, Missouri.

Louisville Work

In the fall of 1969, one of the elders of the Manslick Road church in Louisville called me to ask if I would be interested in talking with them about the work. I had been in a very good meeting a few months before at West End in Bowling Green where his daughter was a member and she had told about the good meeting we had in which sixteen were baptized and six restored. After talking with Bobbie about it, we decided I should go and talk to them. Wilson was soon to be a teenager and we were apprehensive about the school environment and the opportunities he might have to develop in the congregation at Brown Street. I was met at the airport by the three elders. They brought with them a copy of *Truth Magazine* which had my picture in it, so they would be able to recognize me. I preached twice and spent three days, mostly with the elders. They took off from work to provide adequate time for us to talk of many things. During that time we learned a lot about each other and it seemed to them, and to me, that we were on the same page. Preachers and elders make a mistake when they decide to work together without asking lots of questions. In more recent times, there are many more issues at stake than was the case a few years ago. The time to settle and clearly understand salaries, time off for meetings and for family events, to know well what is expected, is beforehand, and not after the truck is unloaded.

During that visit, I had lunch with J. F. Dancer, who was the present preacher at Manslick Road. He had been there for five years. I learned after arriving, that the elders had asked brother Dancer to relocate. They thought it was best for him and for the church. They gave him ample time. When I learned that, I had some misgivings. I told brother Dancer that had I known this before coming, I would probably not

Manslick Road church building in Louisville, Kentucky (1971).

have come. His answer is one I shall never forget. He said, "No, don't feel that way. I have had five good years here. This is a good congregation and the elders are good men. While I don't agree with their judgment about making this change, they do have a right to make this decision. I accepted their judgment about coming here and I will accept it about leaving. I will do everything in my power to leave it in the best shape I can." He told me he hoped I would come and that he was sure we would have a good work. All preachers could learn a lesson from that. Sometimes egos get in the way. In my whole lifetime of preaching, I have not found a nobler spirit than that of J. F. Dancer.

I asked the elders for time to discuss the matter with my wife and children. After doing that and informing the Brown Street elders of our decision, we began preparations to move to Louisville and begin March 1, 1970. That meant we were moving our children in the midst of a school year. That was a difficult adjustment for them and it was the only time we ever moved them during a school year. One of the things which had appealed to me besides the obvious opportunity for growth in the church was the number of good young people and the closeness of their families. There were twenty-five high school students. Parents opened their homes so these young people could do things together in a proper setting. The teenagers sat in a group, at the front, filling several pews. I was asked to teach the high school class on Sunday morning. What a joy that was. For the most part, they were always prepared. They were given special assignments. Out of that class came several preachers, some who now serve as elders and deacons, and women who married such men. Out of that group, I only know of two who fell away. We could not have put our children in a better situation spiritually.

The work grew. Many were baptized and others restored. We began to outgrow the building. We had a balcony which would seat about forty and we were filling that at times and a few Sundays had to put chairs in the vestibule. The pews were close together to seat as many as possible. During a meeting with Cecil Willis, we had over 400 at one service and topped that number in a meeting with Robert Jackson. The elders decided to start a two-preacher arrangement in which we employed for one year a young man just out of college to work with us. While we were there, we worked with Bill Feist and then Gary Henry. Both of them served us well. The elders said that they had noticed that many young men just beginning end up at places where there are no elders and where there has been a history of trouble. Some of these become discouraged and chose not to continue preaching. But they provided the younger man with a good office, right next to mine. They would preach at Manslick Road when I was gone, and sometimes once on Sunday when I was there. They taught classes, did personal work, were responsible for one page in the bulletin, and were treated with respect, while guided in the right direction. It was good for the young men, good for me and for the church, as well. The church took collective pride in watching the growth and improvement of these young men. While Bill Feist was working with us, he began preaching on Sundays at the small church in Hodgenville. When he finished his year with us, he moved there and Manslick Road helped to support him.

During this time, Robert Jackson stayed with us during a meeting. My boys liked Robert. Once, while we were at Brown Street, we took the boys to hear Robert and on the way home, we quizzed them as to what they liked about Robert's sermon. Wilson made some comment about something Robert had said. Martin said, "I liked his cuff links." We had told Robert about that and the last day of his meeting with us, he called both boys into the bedroom. He had laid out some cuff links on the bed and told them they could each choose a pair. They came running out to show us. Well, before Sunday we had to buy both of them a shirt for cuff links. As we walked across the parking lot to the building,

I noticed that both of them had pulled up their coat sleeves enough that those cuff links could be clearly seen.

Bobbie was teaching school at that time and so I did the best I could to prepare breakfast for brother Jackson. He was not too sure about my culinary talents. He kept looking up over his newspaper to see how things were going. One morning I was about to fry him an egg when the egg rolled off in the floor. He looked at the egg and at me. I said, "Robert, how do you feel about scrambled eggs?" He never forgot that and joked with me about it a number of times. During that meeting, Martin obeyed the gospel. Robert Jackson took his confession and I baptized him. The joy of being able to baptize both of our sons was beyond description.

It became obvious that something would have to be done to relieve our crowded condition. A small house was built across the driveway from the preacher's house in which there were two offices, three classrooms, and a work room for printing the bulletin and material for classes. That gave us more classroom space but still did not help the over crowding in the auditorium. There were twenty-five families which had moved into the north end of Bullitt County, the county just south of Louisville. Bullitt County had growing pains and the prospects for a new work in the north end of the county appeared to be very good. The elders called a meeting of all the men and laid out our problem. They said, if we all stayed together, a major building expansion would have to be done and the expense of that would obligate the church financially for several years. On the other hand, if those families who had moved to Bullitt County had any thought of starting a new work, they needed to know about it. They said, if there was enough interest in doing that, they would get behind it and help support a preacher there until the new congregation was able to do so. They suggested that those who had moved to Bullitt County meet together and talk it over. When they did that, they called me into the meeting and asked if we would go with them and help them get started. We thought about it and decided we would go with them. The elders had not expected that, but agreed to find another preacher for Manslick Road and to support me until the new congregation could do so.

A search was made for land and a two acre lot was purchased on Hebron Lane right across from a middle school and later also a high school. It was a great location. We made arrangements to meet temporarily in the cafeteria of the middle school. In late August, 1973, I conducted a two week's tent meeting on the lot we had purchased. The Sunday after the tent meeting ended (in which several were baptized), we met in the middle school as a separate congregation for the first time. Manslick Road deeded the lot to the new Hebron Lane church. It was an entirely peaceful "swarm." We made it clear at Manslick Road, while we were all together, that no pressure was to be employed to persuade anyone either to go or stay. The first Sunday we met as an independent congregation, there were ninety-six present. That relieved the crowded situation at Manslick Road and gave us a good nucleus for the new work. Most of the families were younger people. I was nearly forty-four years old and, except for one man who was six months older, was the oldest man in the new congregation. From the beginning, the work was peaceful. Most of the members had a mind to work and the church grew. Manslick Road brought Julian R. Snell to work with them and that work continued to do well.

Taking on a Heavy Load

In June, 1973, I began editing *Searching The Scriptures*, a monthly periodical. By the time we began that work, we bought a lot in a new sub-division in Bullitt County and built a new house. We moved into it just before the time for the tent meeting to begin. We were starting work with a new congregation. Bobbie had made enough teaching school to enable us to purchase a lot for the new house. We were fortunate to secure a loan at 7¼% interest. Soon after we closed on that loan, the rate went to over 9%. By the time we were ready to start the Hebron Lane building, the rate was over 10%. The house was built by three brethren who were then in business together. They did quality work. All three of those builders are now elders, two of them at Manslick Road and one at Hebron Lane. That house became home for me for twenty-eight years. It was the scene of great happiness and much sorrow, about which I shall write in due time. We bought an American saddle-bred horse named Apache. He was a strong and proud animal with four gaits. Martin became a good horseman. Wilson did not fare as well. They pooled money they had earned cutting grass to buy the horse. But after Wilson sidled Apache into an electric fence and he gave Wilson a wild ride across the pasture, he sold out his interest to Martin. I happened to witness that comical event. Wilson's arms and legs were flapping and flailing and he was yelling, "Whoa, Whoa" loud enough to be heard all over that end of the county and he looked for all the world like Ichabod Crane on his wild ride in *The Legend of Sleep Hollow*. We traded Apache for Kaya, a gentler quarter horse. But, it was good training for them, especially for Martin. He got a job one summer as a wrangler at a dude ranch in Arizona while he was in aeronautical college at Prescott.

Hebron Lane church building in Shepherdsville, Kentucky (1974).

We only worked with the Hebron Lane church for two years. Within one year of our beginning, we were able to move into a new building, and appointed two elders, just before we terminated our work there. I decided that I was away from the local work in meetings more than was good for the Hebron Lane work. The work on the paper created two deadlines a month and much correspondence. It was evident that something had to give. After discussions with my family and with the elders at Expressway in Louisville, the decision was made to embark on a new chapter in which I would hold gospel meetings for nine months each year and conduct Bible classes at Expressway during the months of December, January, and February. We continued to live in Bullitt County. Leaving Hebron Lane was our own choice. The brethren were gracious about it and secured the services of Everett Hardin who did excellent work for the ten years he was with them.

Wilson went to Florida College about the time we began our work with Expressway. He never lived at home again. Martin was still in high school and I had misgivings about being gone so much while he was still living at home. I had long talks with him and with Bobbie before making this decision. While he assured me he understood the importance of what I would be doing, still, we both missed a great deal. Had he been unruly I could not have done it. Bobbie's attitude was, "You go preach the gospel and I'll keep the home fires burning." She quit her teaching job and took on the business management for *Searching The Scriptures*.

The Expressway Years

We began our work under the new arrangement with a gospel meeting at Expressway. From then on for the next ten years, I was in meetings for nine months (ranging from eighteen to twenty-three a year) and taught four or five classes a week during the winter months. There were classes on Monday nights and Friday mornings in addition to Sunday mornings and Wednesday nights. I taught a Thursday night class at Valley Station during that first year of work with Expressway. We covered a wide range of subject matter in those classes. We studied Sermon Preparation and Delivery, How to Study the Bible, New Testament Introduction, Between the Testaments, Evangelism, Jeremiah, Daniel, Ezra and Nehemiah, The Minor Prophets, 1 and 2 Corinthians, Revelation, Secular Humanism, Denominational Doctrines, and other subjects and books of the Bible. Many preachers, young and older, plus elders and other members came from throughout the area. Steve Wolfgang was the local preacher during part of that time and Jerry Parks for the rest of it. Both men were congenial co-workers and our association was pleasant in every way. For a few months before brother Parks came, I filled the pulpit at Expressway while home between meetings. The elders there were supportive of the work we did and when I decided to leave Expressway, they told me and the congregation this was entirely my decision and, as far as they were concerned, I could have continued in the same arrangement for a long time to come.

One of the strengths of the Expressway work has always been their emphasis on improving their Bible classes. They would project several years ahead, chart it on a large poster board to see where there might be gaps that needed to be filled in teaching. The class I enjoyed teaching the most was the Friday morning winter class. We scheduled it for two hours each time. After an hour we gave them a five minute break, and then started again. That cut review time in half and enabled us to study longer books in the Bible in a shorter time span. Those who came to this class were serious students who came to learn. They did not complain about the length of the class. The Monday night class took on the aura of one night of a gospel meeting. We had to have it in the auditorium to accommodate the number who came. Many attended from churches in the area and some drove in from 100 miles away. Many congregations do not allow enough time for Bible classes. While it is not practical to have classes of two hours all the time, many are satisfied with twenty-five or thirty minutes. When I am in a meeting where that is the case, I usually ask them what they have against studying the Bible? Such classes as we had required much extra study for me but it was well worth the effort. During fall gospel meetings, I would read and work on material for the winter classes. For many years I formed the habit of reading at least one book during a meeting. This practice served well in preparing for those classes.

We had a Baptist preacher and his wife to attend a Friday morning class on the book of Daniel. He had debated Clinton D. Hamilton at Expressway some years before and was an elderly man at the time he studied Daniel with us. He said he was curious to see how someone who was not premillennial would teach the book of Daniel. His questions and comments in class were not confrontational and actually helped the study.

The Expressway church was the result of a tragic division at the large Taylor Boulevard congregation. At one time that was the largest congregation in the state of Kentucky. Grover Stevens preached there when they numbered better than 800 members. When Harold Hazelip came to work with them, he brought much talent and promise to the work. At first he took a firm stand for the truth. I heard a speech he made at the Florida College lectures on the "Work of the Church." It was excellent. But in time, he, along with his brother Woodrow, Bill Humble, H. A. Fincher, and L. Wesley Jones, changed directions and tried to take the churches where they were preaching along with them. At Taylor Boulevard, only one elder, L. L. Dukes, and two deacons, Harold Byers and Paul Woodward, took a stand against institutionalism. The congregation was divided in sentiment. The liberal element sought a legal injunction against the rest to force them to vacate the building. While that was going on, Robert Jackson came for a meeting. Several who witnessed what took place all told the same story. Some of the liberals paraded back and forth across the front to create distraction while Robert was preaching. One man threatened Robert with a knife. Brother Dukes rescued him. Some of the women sat up on the back of the pews on the back row and kicked the seat with their high heels to make noise to keep people from hearing Robert. On one occasion a brother came into the pulpit and literally tore the coat off of Paul Woodward. The depositions taken by the court have been published in a booklet about the trouble there. They are sad to read, but they are a good sample of the kind of ungodliness that sometimes took place during those hectic years. The court ruled against the liberal element and they made a settlement with the ones who began the Expressway work. The majority went with the liberals, but 200 left to form Expressway. They engaged James P. Needham to work with them. He actually began his work before the legal actions were taken. His work there was outstanding and the church at

Expressway became known far and wide during the time brother Needham worked there.

It is sometimes said by younger men who did not experience what went on in those years, that there were bad attitudes on both sides. I am certain that in frustration, some said things that would have been better not said. But in my own knowledge and experience, I do not know of a case where the more conservative element instigated a lawsuit over property. I know for a fact that many brethren pleaded with the more liberal element to keep the door open for study. In all too many cases, it became a matter of having to line up or get out. Why write about all this? Because some have been under false impressions about what happened in the 1950's and 1960's. When error first raises its head, it may appear sweet and innocent, but when it does not get its way, it turns ferocious and scratches and claws at whatever is in the way. I, personally, have been on the receiving end of some of that sweet, innocent treatment.

A landmark event in the history of the work in Louisville was the debate between A. C. Grider and Guy N. Woods. Brother Grider came to preach at Preston Highway in Louisville and began to oppose what men like Hazelip, Humble, Fincher, and Jones were trying to do. He was having such an effect, that they prevailed on Guy N. Woods to come and debate A. C. Grider in an effort to shut him up. The result of that debate was that many brethren got their eyes open to what was happening and to the Bible principles at stake. That is why, to this day, the institutional churches in Louisville are outnumbered. Every faithful church in the area owes a debt of gratitude to A. C. Grider.

My work at Expressway was not to end before the storm clouds of sadness had gathered above me and descended in all their fury.

Chapter 10

Till Death Do Us Part

When Bobbie and I fell in love, planned and dreamed of our life together, neither of us could envision what it would mean to lose the other to death. When the thought crossed my mind later, I somehow assumed that I would be the one to leave her behind. We bought insurance with that in mind. We both understood that "it is appointed unto man once to die and after that the judgment" (Heb. 9:27). I often quoted that passage in sermons. On occasion, we discussed what songs we would want sung at our funerals. Each of us told the other that we would want the one who was left behind to remarry and to go on with life, depending on our age and health. But it is hard for healthy young people to truly face the reality of that event. Before Wilson was born, Bobbie did write a letter which I found while she was yet in the hospital in Bergen, Norway. In that letter she spoke of the possibility that something might go wrong and she wanted me to know her mind about several things in case the child survived and she did not. But, with that exception, we did not dwell on the subject.

It is gracious on the Lord's part that we do not know what tomorrow may bring. Every day God gives us is a special treasure and should be lived to the fullest. I was in a meeting at Russellville, Alabama, working with J. F. Dancer and staying in his home, when Bobbie called me. It was early August, 1982. She had found a lump on her breast, had it removed and analyzed, and had just received the diagnosis. It was malignant. When she said that word, it cut me to the heart. The doctor insisted that a mastectomy should be performed as soon as possible. We were having day services during the meeting in Russellville and somehow, I spoke that morning, but closed my part of the meeting and headed home to Brooks. It was an anxious trip. I found Bobbie worried but composed.

We met with her doctor the next day and she had surgery the following day. Two lymph nodes were also affected. It had spread, we just did not know how far. She handled the chemotherapy very well, though it made her hair fall out. She wore a wig which looked so much like her real hair that many could not tell the difference. The twenty-six radiation treatments were hard for her. The first year, things went very well and we had hopes of conquering this terrible enemy. Thankfully, great

Connie and Bobbie Adams (1983).

progress has been made in treating that form of cancer, but early detection is still critical. Her optimistic, cheerful attitude amazed doctors and made things easier for all of us. If she ever felt sorry for herself, she kept it within. I asked her if she had ever said or even thought, "Why me, Lord?" She said, "No, I am no better or different from anyone else."

I kept thinking we were going to overcome it. Yet, in the back of my mind, I crossed "What if?" bridges. The last few months were very hard for her and for those of us who stood by and tried to help. Her mother, Virginia Colley, lived with us, and those days were especially hard for her. Bobbie was in and out of the hospital. Fluid built up around her lungs and had to be drained so she could breath. In the spring of 1985, I cancelled three months of meetings so I could remain by her side. The Eastland church in Louisville was between preachers and they graciously asked me to preach for them on Sundays and teach a Wednesday night class and paid me a full salary for those three months, though I was not able to attend to many things a local preacher would do. The last time we were in the hospital, I stayed all night with her on Saturday. We read the Bible, prayed together, talked a little while, and watched a final four NCAA game. She slept well. I had taken a suit in case I went to Eastland to preach. The next morning, she said she felt better and urged me to get dressed and go on to preach. Her mother was coming to stay with her anyhow. I said, "Are you sure?" She said, "I'm sure. Go preach, and do it right."

Upon returning to the hospital, as soon as I got off the elevator, I saw flurried activity around the door of her room. I ran down there and found the doctor, nurses, and attendants working feverishly. Mrs. Colley (we called her Nana) stood by in stunned silence. Bobbie was in a coma and soon after I entered the room, breathed her last. At the ripe old age of fifty-two, she broke the bonds of mortality and her noble spirit soared to yonder's world to await the resurrection of all the dead. We had watched her struggle so much for the past few weeks that I felt a sense of relief for her, but there are no words to describe the ache which overwhelmed me. I tried to comfort Nana. Her doctor lost his composure for a few moments. When I could speak, I assured him that he and his partner in practice had done all they could, but there are just some things man cannot do. I called Harold and Esther Byers from Expressway and they came right away and stayed with me until her body was removed to the funeral home. During that time, I called our two sons in Maryland. Our two daughters-in-law had just returned home after spending several days with us to help Bobbie and to help in the office of *Searching The Scriptures*. I called the elders at Eastland and told them I would like to go to Expressway that night and they said they would take care of getting someone to speak in my place. By the time Nana and I got back to the house at Brooks, a crowd had gathered. Good neighbors and brethren were there to help in whatever way they might be needed. After awhile, I excused myself to prepare to go to services at 6 o'clock at Expressway. That was the best thing I could have done. Everything about the service was uplifting to my sagging spirit. The handshakes and embraces from so many spoke eloquently of their love and understanding. What do people do in times of such great loss without brethren in Christ?

How many came to the visitation at Heady's Funeral Home in the Okolona area of Louisville, I do not know. The lines were long as people waited to view her remains and to speak words of comfort to us. Many preachers, elders and their wives came, as well as members from many congregations in the area. Our printer and his wife drove five hours from Berne, Indiana. Dear friends came from Atlanta. The Expressway building was filled to overflowing on April 2, 1985. Brethren came from several states, including my dear friend H. E. Phillips, who flew from Tampa. I requested that he and Tom O'Neal sit with the family. We asked two old friends,Weldon Warnock and Dee Bowman, to speak. Both of them had to interrupt a meeting to come. Weldon spoke of personal ties and read an article Bobbie had written which was published in *Truth Magazine* and *Searching The Scriptures* entitled, "The Blessings of a Preacher's Wife." We had congregational singing. Yes, the boys and I were able to sing, too. A Catholic neighbor, who was present for the service, asked me if it was a requirement for membership in the church of Christ that you be a good singer. Dee spoke, in his eloquent manner, of the various faces of death.

We laid her to rest in the Hebron Cemetery in Bullitt County, in sight of the Hebron Lane church building. My name is also chiseled on the stone marker awaiting only the date of my departure. A. C. and Hallie Grider bought burial lots with only one grave between theirs and ours. Brother Grider told me that on the resurrection day, they would know somebody "right away." April 2 that year was as lovely a day as Kentucky can provide at that season of the year.

The wise man wrote, "It is better to go to the house of mourning than to the house of feasting" (Eccl. 7:2). Why is that true? (1) "The living will lay it to his heart." It is impossible to go to a funeral and not think about life and death. It is an ideal time to preach the gospel. The presence of death has already sobered the audience. It is a time of introspection. "When will it be my time?" "What will they say about me?" "Will there be anyone who will care enough to come?" (2) We are brought face to face with our own mortality at a funeral. Our earthly sojourn is not permanent and we are not invincible. (3) Funerals bring out the best in some people. Oh yes, there are some relatives who have so little respect for the dead that they act like heathens in airing their family squabbles. But there are many who open their hearts and their wallets to do something kind for those who are hurting. Food is prepared and brought in abundance. Friends or neighbors step in to make phone calls for you, run errands, and help in so many ways. One neighbor offered to wash my car. So many have bought into the Calvinistic notion that man is inherently sinful, that his very nature is corrupt. No, no, man does not have a sinful nature any more than he has a righteous nature. We are born with freedom of choice. Do humans do wrong? Yes, because they chose to do so. Do they do good? Yes, because they chose to do so. It is this power of human choice that we have to assume when we preach the gospel to people. Can they reject it? To be sure. But, they can also accept it to the saving of their souls.

(4) Funerals help us to count our blessings. The next time you attend a funeral and some man is burying his wife, be thankful that you still have yours and go home and tell her how much you love her and need her. The same goes for a woman who has lost a husband, or children a parent, or parents a child. Value these relationships and make the most of them. (5) Funerals are therapeutic. They are emotional shock absorbers. They also bring closure. It is my view that it is healthy to be able to view the body, when that is possible, or at least have it present. The coldest, emptiest funerals I have ever attended have been those where the dead had been cremated and there was perhaps a picture left to view. A visible corpse lets you know that this is real and helps to accept that sad reality.

After They All Go Home

After a death, plans have to be made for a funeral. Relatives and friends have to be notified. For two or three days, one moves in a daze from one thing to another which must be done. But then, when it is all over and everyone has gone home, you must face the reality of life without the one you lost. That is the hard part. Bobbie's presence seemed to be everywhere in the house we had built at Brooks. Everything was a reminder. The house itself was an early Virginia design which she had chosen. I found it difficult just to walk through the house surrounded by so many memories. There was a guest room for which she had made the curtains and bedspread, and the fireplace in the den where we had spent such happy hours. I used to sing a song, which to this day, I am not able to sing without choking with emotion. There was a verse which said:

> She slipped into the silence of my dreams last night.
> Wandering from room to room, turning on each light.
> Her laughter spills like water from the rivers to the sea.
> And I'm swept away from sadness, clinging to her memory.
> Sweet memories, sweet memories
> And I'm swept away from sadness clinging to her memory.

For a long time, my office was my refuge. I came close to becoming a workaholic. When it became necessary to leave the house for some errand, I tried to find reasons to delay returning. Bedtime was difficult. That room was so empty. Each night seemed to be a thousand years long. But daylight always came. Prayers, long prayers, drew me closer to the real source of all comfort. I made a decision soon to dispose of her clothes. My sister-in-law, Wilma, said she would be honored to have them and Nana agreed that would be the best thing to do with them. Cleaning out her closet was hard, but it, too, was therapeutic. I folded each garment and placed the garments in boxes, and relived occasions when she wore that dress, skirt, blouse, or suit. Yes, I cried a river. Nana would not just break down and let it all out. But I did.

Learning To Live Again

While Nana helped with cooking and what things she was able to do, the insistent demands of everyday existence forced me into doing many things I was not accustomed to doing. I was reared in a culture where the man took care of outdoor chores (plowing, cutting wood, tending livestock, work in the yard and fields), and woman handled domestic duties. My cooking skills were minimal. I could occasionally fry an egg without breaking the yolk. When Nana had to be occupied away from the house, I would go to a fast food place for lunch, mainly because there were people there and I did not feel totally alone. Laundry was a whole new world. The first time I tried to wash and dry clothes, I was amazed and baffled by the choices. How was I to know the difference between cotton, linen, and permapress? Cold water for this and hot water for that. I decided I might have to go back to college to learn how to do my laundry. I could take a chain saw, go into the woods and cut firewood, or cut up kindling with an axe. I knew how to milk cows, groom and saddle or hitch up a horse, feed pigs, or pitch hay. But this was a different world for me. On top of all that, Bobbie was the family book keeper. She always knew to the penny how much we had in the bank. I did not even know how to balance the checkbook. She prepared information for the accountant for our tax work which became more complicated after we began publishing *Searching The Scriptures*. I had to work out a schedule of what bills were due and when. The divine truth that "it is not good for the man, that he should be alone" has many ramifications.

There were unexpected social adjustments. I found myself excluded from events which were planned for couples. One is not a couple. While family and friends were going on with life as usual, I was struggling to balance memories with the demands of day-to-day living. Then there was a new problem. Well meaning friends sometimes wanted to play "cupid." Bobbie died in March. I had cancelled meetings through May. But in the very first meeting in June, I came face to face with this problem. This continued for some time. I would be invited for dinner (which is normal during meetings), but there would be a widow or other single woman also invited and the seating arrangement. . . . Well, you can figure that out. I had several phone calls from friends which usually began with, "Now brother Connie, I don't mean to meddle in your business, but I know this wonderful lady. . . ." I received mail from widows who were on the mailing list of *Searching The Scriptures* offering their sympathy and understanding. Some were subtle while others were more aggressive. You may be wondering the same thing Nannie Yater Tant expressed when J. D. Tant was courting her and told her he could have his pick among women. She replied, "Pray tell, what is the attraction?" I wondered that myself. But it all brought to mind something which Roy Cogdill told me after Lorraine died and he married Nita. He said, "The brethren will marry you off if you will let them." At first, I was annoyed by these attempts. Then I decided to take it in stride with humor. It did not take long to spot a "set up."

It did take awhile to adjust to my new status. I continued to wear my wedding ring for several months. But one day, as I was driving to town, the sun glinted off that ring and I said aloud, "I'm not married." Why that had not fully registered, I do not know. It does not take long to become satiated with loneliness. For a while, I would go to the cemetery and hold one-sided conversations with a grave stone. I would watch couples my own age at a mall, a restaurant and at services, as they obviously enjoyed being together, and would have to fight against the sin of envy. If I could just find someone who really understood and to whom I could unburden my troubled heart, maybe just talking about it would help.

Enter Bobby Hughes

I first met Tom and Bobby Hughes when we lived in Akron, Ohio. I held meetings in North Ridgeville, west of Cleveland and at Berea, where Tom Hughes was an elder. During a meeting at Berea in the fall of 1965, I had dinner one night with the Hughes family. Bobby does not remember it. No wonder, for they had six children, three boys and three girls, and I was just another preacher invited for a meal during a meeting. Tom was an unusually bright man. Dee Bowman once said of him, "You can ask Tom what time it is, and he can tell you how to make a clock." He was deeply committed to the truth and, along with Les Stricklin (the other elder at Berea), determined to keep that church headed in the right direction. The Hughes family not only attended several meetings in which I preached, but also visited meetings at Brown Street. Tom was one of the best Bible class teachers I ever met. In fact, he conducted several weekend meetings on teacher training.

We moved to Louisville in 1970 and the Hughes family came in 1974. Bobby's parents were members at Expressway and they placed membership there and soon became very active in the work. In 1975 we placed membership at Expressway and worshipped there when at home between meetings and taught the winter classes already described. We sat on the row right in front of Tom and Bobby. The two, Bobbie and Bobby, became good friends. Tom ran his own business (he was a consultant to the printing industry), and would take off from work each Friday morning during the winter to attend those classes. We often had lunch together on Sundays or after the Friday morning class. They even asked us to serve as legal guardian for Kimberley, their youngest child, should something happen to both of them, and we agreed. Tom was diagnosed with prostate cancer. It was well advanced by the time it was discovered. He lived a little more that four years, defying all expectations from his doctors. Bobby drove him to seminars all over the country and pushed him in a wheel chair the last year and a half. I remember once when Bobbie was in the hospital that Bobby came pushing Tom in that chair to see her. For a short time, Tom wrote a column on "Teaching" in *Seachcing The Scriptures*. He died in a cancer hospital in Zion, Illinois in December, 1982 at the age of sixty. When Bobby got home from Zion, Harold and Esther Byers and Bobbie and I were at the house waiting for her. I preached at Tom's funeral. Bobby and Bobbie often sat together at Expressway when I was away in meetings. Our good friend, Hall Davis, who lived in Louisville for a few years and attended Expressway, referred to the two of them as Bobbie Joe and Bobby Jack. One Sunday they both appeared in identical green blazers and accused each other of trying to look "preppie."

One Sunday afternoon, in a moment of distress, I picked up the phone and called Bobby and asked her if she would meet me at a Mexican restaurant after services that night and that I just needed to talk to someone who knew what I was going through. At the moment, courting was not on my mind. The conversation centered on Bobbie and coping with grief. Other such meetings followed. One day when we were driving around and talking, I said, "Now, I want you to know, we are not courting.""Of course not," she replied with a twinkle in her eye. As it became obvious to me (she knew already) that we were, indeed, courting, we knew we had to have time to sort out a lot of things before friends and brethren knew we were interested in each other. We knew that the very minute we were seen together at a restaurant or some other place, they would have us married whether we meant to be or not. So, we ate at some pretty nice places where we did not think we would likely run into brethren. We both had been married for nearly thirty-five years and had many memories. We decided that with seventy total years of married life to begin, we ought to know something about it. She had six children and I had two. All of them were grown and away from home. Once, at a fancy restaurant in downtown Louisville, I told her I had something very serious to ask her but that it was something we really ought to talk about. She took me seriously and said, "What is it?" I asked, "How many children do you think we ought to have?" Without hesitation she said, "Get lost." I was fifty-five and she was two years older. The first time we sat together at Expressway, we could sense that everyone noticed. I gave her a ring on Halloween (whether it was Trick or Treat, you will have to ask her) and we went to a meeting that night at Expressway to hear Glenn Seaton. There was a lot of excitement after the service.

I wrote a letter to Donna, Rick, Gordon, Kurt, Elynn, and Kimberley and told them I would not attempt to replace their father but that I loved their mother and would do everything in my power to provide for her and protect her. I talked to both of my boys. It has been hard for all of them to adjust to changing relationships, but they have all tried and have been gracious. When we asked Wilson to say the ceremony, he, at first, said he was not sure he could do it, but after thinking about it, agreed to do it and did a good job of it. We were married in a quiet ceremony attended by family and only a few others. We went to the Opryland Hotel in Nashville for a few days. We had told nobody except my mother where we would be, but Harold Byers (who was my best man) and Wilson figured it out. Esther Byers called the hotel right after we left town and asked to speak with us. They were told that we had not checked in *yet*. That gave it away. When we reached the hotel room, there were some roses on a table with a note which said, "We are following and watching." We went back down to the desk and I asked if they could protect celebrities from nuisance calls. They said they did that all of the time. I said, "Well, we are celebrities and we just got married." They assured us they would handle it. Calls were headed off at the desk and messages were taken which were given to us when we requested them. Bob Owen left a message saying that he was hurt that we would leave the state when he was in a meeting seventy-five miles from Louisville. Jim and Paige Deason wanted to know if they could leave the children with us while they did some shopping in Nashville. Some of our *Truth Magazine* friends left a message which said, "We know where you are, but at your age, we can't imagine why you are there." Well, what are friends for? Our honeymoon trip actually lasted one month, but that included two gospel meetings. After leaving Nashville, we went to Gulfport, Mississippi for a meeting. That was followed by an open week during which we went to New Orleans (it did not take long to get enough of that place) and Corpus Christi, Texas. Then we had another meet-

ing at West Columbia, Texas.

But everyone was not pleased with this marriage. We had waited a year after Bobbie died (and there is good reason to wait long enough for emotions to settle), but Nana thought it was too soon. My boys told me that she would have felt the same if we had waited five years. She decided to rent an apartment, even though we had told her she could continue to live with us. Not many women would have agreed to live in the same house with her husband's former mother-in-law. Nana really liked Bobby and Bobby genuinely loved

Connie and Bobby on their wedding day in 1986.

Nana. She spent a lot of time at our house and we did the best we could to see that she had what she needed. I often took her to lunch, to appointments with her doctor, took time to play "Phase Ten" with her (a card game which she dearly loved), she made trips with us, and was regarded as part of the family.

Some of the close friends Bobbie and I had were not pleased either. Much to my surprise, they treated me as if I had somehow betrayed Bobbie. To them, it had been just a short time since she had died. They could not know how long the nights had been and how desolate life had become alone. But some brethren were elated at this turn of events. Bobby and Tom had visited brethren in Italy and helped finance some work there. Some of the Italian brethren had visited in their home as well as ours. Bobbie and I had been to Italy twice to work among the brethren. When the news reached them that we had married, they sent messages of congratulations and said they had been praying for this to happen. Come to think of it, I didn't have a chance! But some friends wondered how you could so soon forget one you loved and lived with for nearly thirty-five years. Of course, you never forget. You don't want to forget. When I met Barbara Rose Colley, I built a special place in my heart for her. When she died, the memories lingered, but then I built another special room in my heart for Bobby. In fact, it has been an advantage to both of us to have known and loved the spouses we lost to cancer. We can freely talk about Tom or Bobbie without feelings of resentment, jealousy, or comparison. We had a finished basement in our house at Brooks and turned a large room into a family picture gallery. One whole wall was covered with Hughes and Adams family pictures and another wall with pictures of all of our grandchildren. Bobby is the only grandmother my children's children have known or can remember and I am the only grandfather most of Bobby's grandchildren have known. We treat them all alike.

What's in a Name?

My story would not be complete without comment on my name and that of the two wives. First, I was named for Connie Mack, a renowned baseball player and manager at the time of my birth. My parents never could have imagined the problems that would cause me. In fact, as long as my mother lived (to nearly ninety-two), she did not see why that was ever a problem. But from the time I started to public school, it created conflict. That continued through high school, though playing basketball mitigated it somewhat. Other boys would say, "You've got a girl's name." I was afflicted with a hot temper, especially when I was younger, and was often in fights and scuffles, usually over being teased about my name. But there is always something to learn. Before you tie into a fellow you had better look him up and down first, or else you will get your clock cleaned. But the problem did not go away in adulthood. I get mail addressed to "Miss Connie Adams" or worse yet, "Ms Connie Adams." Brethren have had some problems advertising meetings because of my name. I try to tell them to either use a picture, or else refer to me as "Mr." Brethren are often asked if they are having a woman preacher for a meeting. Brethren usually know me but others do not. Often, when it is my turn to be called into a doctor's office, the aide will announce "Mrs. Adams" and I just get up and grin through it. One time I was being admitted to a hospital in Gainesville, Florida for some tests. When I appeared, the aide asked, "You're Connie Adams?" Then she picked up the phone and called a nurse on the floor where I was to be admitted and said, "Hey, we're gonna' have to reassign rooms for Connie Adams. He's a man!"

Connie and Bobby at their house at Brooks, KY (1988).

Bobbie's name was really Barbara and Bobbie was just a nickname which everyone used but her mother. But people still got us confused and assumed that Bobbie was the husband and Connie the wife. But Bobby's name is really that – Bobby. Brethren often misspell it in announcements about classes she is to teach for women. She suffered the same identity problems at school as I did. She regularly gets mail addressed to "Mr." Bobby Adams. We sometimes have fun with telephone solicitors. But neither of us got to vote on our names. They are what they are. But I do have some advice for parents who search through books and old movies to give their children unusual names. Don't! Children are often unmerciful. When you give your child a name which can be twisted into a joke or which is grossly out of the ordinary, you will expose that child to a lifetime of teasing and vexation. But I have had one unique advantage in being married to the two precious women God has given me. I am the only man I know named Connie who has been married to two women named Bobbie (or Bobby). And I have never called my wife the wrong name.

Bobby and I (at this writing) have been married twenty-three years. They have been wonderful years and have passed all too soon. When I see the unhappy marriages of so many and the tragic divorces, I am made to thank the Lord for giving me the two treasures He has granted me. Both have been devoted to the Lord and to me. Both have encouraged me in the work of preaching the gospel. Neither one has ever tried to hinder me in that work. Bobby has traveled with me extensively in gospel meeting work and has often been called on to teach classes for women. Preachers and elders have often misread the degree of interest which many women have in such classes and attendance has always been more than they expected. She has taught these classes in several countries, using an interpreter when necessary. In the Philippines she had classes of from 75 to 500 women. My first Bobbie adjusted well to the several moves we made and did not complain about pulling up roots and putting down new ones. She had no patience with whining, complaining preacher's wives or with mothers who did not want their daughters to marry preachers, or with preacher's wives who could not move out of the same county where their mother lived. My second Bobby has adjusted well to making ourselves at home in motel rooms or in the homes of those who have kept us during meetings. Ever since we married, we have been in meetings every year from the first of March to the end of November, usually two a month. There have been several overseas preaching trips. Every now and then some sister will wrinkle her nose and ask, "Do you really like all that?" They are often surprised by her answer of "I love it." Some wonder if she does not get "bored" traveling. Well, no, we both do this work because we believe the Lord wants us to do it and we have not stopped long enough to even ask whether or not we like it. What does that have to do with anything? As for boredom, that is a state of mind which is regulated by the will. We have found either beauty or something interesting about the changing landscapes we see. The desert has a special beauty. Have you ever been in Arizona when the cactus was in bloom? The seashore is fascinating and speaks of the power of God to form these giant beds of water and to determine their boundaries. There is majesty about the mountains. The prophets often used the symbolism of mountains to describe governments and rulers. It is a sad commentary on our times that parents have to buy vehicles equipped with video games or movies to keep their children occupied as they travel through the wondrous world God has made. I have broken my grandchildren from complaining about being "bored." When they say that, we find a job for them so they will have something to "do." "Bored" is a bad word at our house!

Don't get me wrong. We love to be in our own home and sleep in our own bed. But we do not consider it a sacrifice to be allowed to go to various places and tell the old, old story. To do that, you must first get there. We have thought of writing a book on "Rest Stops We Have Known." We enjoy uninterrupted time to talk. We sometimes listen to music (all kinds except rap and rock). We love to listen to tapes or CD's of hymn singing and sing along. When we have several hours to travel in a day, we have a morning routine which is special to us. As soon as we get on the open road, Bobby reads several chapters from the Bible. Over the years, we have read through the whole Bible several times just in the early morning of travel. That has been special.

Twice I have promised "Till death do us part" and meant it both times. I thank my God for Bobbie 1 and Bobby 2 and the great blessing they have been to my life and work.

Chapter 11

The Gospel Is For All

Jesus charged His apostles with the momentous task of going into all the world and preaching the gospel to every creature in all the nations. Those baptized were then to be taught to "observe all things whatsoever I have commanded you." What did He command them to do? Why, they were to go teach all nations (see Matt. 28:18-20; Mark 16:15-16; Luke 24:47-49). Paul instructed Timothy to "teach faithful men who shall be able to teach others also" (2 Tim. 2:2). The early Christians took this charge seriously. When persecution scattered them from Jerusalem, they "went everywhere preaching the word" (Acts 8:4). They filled Jerusalem with the doctrine, then took the message throughout Judea, and then to Samaria. It spread up the coast to Antioch of Syria whence it was hurled into its world-wide orbit. Paul said, ". . . their sound went into all the earth, and their words unto the ends of the world" (Rom. 10:18). He also spoke of "the word of the truth of the gospel; which is come unto you, as it is in all the world; and bringeth forth fruit. . ." (Col. 1:5-6). This was accomplished within thirty years of the beginning on Pentecost. They did it without a printing press, the modern means of communication, and without the methods of travel which we take for granted. The love of Christ constrained them (2 Cor. 5:14). The fear of eternal punishment evoked their mercy upon the lost (2 Cor. 5:11). Should we not be driven by the same motives which stirred them to action?

As mentioned in an earlier chapter, the pictures and stories of preaching in Alaska which I heard as a teenager from Arley Moore at Hopewell, Virginia, stirred my heart to want to preach Christ in as many places as possible in my lifetime. Early in life, I prayed for the Lord to open doors of opportunity to do that. He has abundantly answered those prayers. Norway was our first experi-

You Are Cordially Invited To Hear
EVANGELIST

CONNIE W. ADAMS

of Newbern, Tenn.

CHURCH OF CHRIST

869-4th Ave. East, Owen Sound

In a Special 8 Days Meeting

MAY 6th to 13th

Each Night at 8 o'clock
Sunday Services at 11 a.m. and 7.30 p.m.
2.45 on CFOS, Sunday, May 6th and 13th

A HEARTY WELCOME AWAITS YOU

Meeting announcement, Owen Sound, Ontario (1961).

ence at preaching overseas. While we were there, I had opportunity to preach in gospel meetings in Sweden and Denmark and to preach in Switzerland and in Paris, France. One such meeting was unique. In Aarhus, Denmark, I preached in Norwegian and they understood me. Norwegian and Danish are similar, though Danish has more of a guttural sound. Keep in mind that my Norwegian was flavored with a southern accent. The preaching occasion in Paris was also unique. At the morning service that day, A. C. Pullias, who was then the president of David Lipscomb College, was asked to speak and I was invited to preach that evening. The workers in Paris were from Texas and were supported by a sponsoring church. They showed us much kindness. At a gathering in the home of one of the preachers, they discovered, to their dismay, that I was an "anti." They did not know that there were any "antis" who were involved in foreign evangelism. Remember also, that the lines of fellowship had not all been tightly drawn everywhere. On that same trip, I spoke one Sunday in Zurich, Switzerland where Heinrich Blum was then preaching. We had been students together at Florida Christian College and he interpreted for me into German.

The Canadian Connection

In 1961, I preached in the first of over forty meetings in Ontario, Canada. I traveled by bus from Newbern, Tennessee to Owen Sound, on Georgian Bay. John Whitfield was the dedicated preacher there. That was the first of three meetings at that place. Most of the congregations in Ontario were small.

Brother Whitfield was a staunchly conservative man. He was then serving on the board of Great Lakes Christian College at Beamsville, Ontario and was much concerned over the direction it was taking. Well known brethren of a liberal persuasion were being brought in for lecture programs and to teach and his lone voice was being drowned out by the rest. There were times when the Whitfields did not have adequate support and John would pick apples and do odd jobs to make ends meet. His wife was a godly and gracious lady.

While in the meeting at Owen Sound, Art and Lillian Corbett from Jordan, Ontario came up to support the meeting. They were prominent farmers from the fertile Niagara peninsula, about forty miles from Buffalo, New York. Art was one of the elders at Jordan. He and Lillian had been converted by Roy E. Cogdill who had spent several summers preaching from place to place in Ontario. While they had had a private study with brother Cogdill, they responded to the invitation at the first public service they attended where brother Cogdill was preaching. What a treasure they were! The meeting with the Corbetts began a friendship which lasted until their death. Through them, we were invited to Jordan and have conducted numerous meetings there and in that general area. The church at Jordan then numbered about 175-200 and for years they helped support much of the work in Ontario. They underwrote several of my meetings in Canada. Strong ties were formed with the faithful brethren in that country and precious memories linger.

One meeting at Jordan stands out in memory. It was in January and we had heavy snow during part of it. Harold Tabor, an old friend from Atlanta days (and later the librarian at Florida College), was teaching at Great Lakes Christian College, and was invited to lead singing during the meeting. While I was preaching, the power went out. I continued preaching and, at the time of the invitation, Harold led the song from memory and brethren stood at the front of the aisles with flashlights. Four people responded and requested baptism. One brother suggested that we ought to turn the lights out every night.

During one meeting at Bancroft, I took Wilson and three other young men along to help. We all stayed in the home of Peter and Judy McPherson and the boys spent each morning canvassing the town to hand out literature and invite people to the meeting. It helped to broaden their horizons and realize the need for gospel work elsewhere. During another meeting at Bancroft, Peter baptized a young woman, her mother, and her grandmother, the same night. You don't often see three generations obey the gospel at the same time.

Connie walking the plank across a stream on the way to preach at Kawit, Pagadian City, Mindanao (1971).

Work in the Philippines

The Lord's work in the Philippines began in the late 1920's when George Benson (later the president of Harding College) had to layover for a few weeks on his way to China. He spent that time on the island of Mindoro and established a work at Roxas. Others came to work and the cause grew. Even during the Japanese occupation of the Philippines during World War II, brother Diosdado Menor baptized over 200 on Mindoro. He was a school teacher but spent his time between school sessions preaching all over Mindoro and in Luzon. Some of the early work was tinged with premillennialism. Then after the war, there were brethren who came under the sponsoring church plan. A college was founded at Baguio City on Luzon and also at Zamboanga City on Mindanao. Romulo Agduma in Mindanao and Victorio Tibayan in Luzon became acquainted with the *Gospel Guardian* through the efforts of Jady Copeland. Juanito Balbin, then the young librarian at the school in Zamboanga City began to have questions about some of the practices of the brethren. In 1970, Roy E. Cogdill and Cecil Willis made a trip to Luzon, Mindoro, and Mindanao. They were well received. There was a legal problem about churches owning property in the name of Church of Christ, since there was a prominent sect, *Iglesia ni Christo*, already registered with that name. With brother Cogdill's legal experience it was thought he might be able to help and he could did. The work was publicized in *Truth Magazine* and much interest was generated thereby.

Meanwhile, J. T. Smith and I were working in Louisville, he with the Gardner Lane church and I with the Manslick Road church. J. T. had left the institutional cause and had written a tract explaining why he

Connie baptizing nine at M'lang, Cotabato, Mindanao (1971).

did so. A well-known, older preacher in Mindanao, Eusebio Lacauta, read that tract, and wrote J. T. challenging him to a debate on the sponsoring church and church support of benevolent institutions. Cecil Willis had already been encouraging me to go to the Philippines, so when J. T. asked me to go with him and moderate in the debate, I was ready and willing to do so. We planned to spend a month, dividing our time between Luzon, Mindoro, and Mindanao.

The debate was arranged and was to be conducted in the meeting house at M'Lang, Cotabato Province on Mindanao. There would be four nights, two each on the two propositions. During the daytime, a lectureship would be conducted in the same building. J. T. spoke each morning but was given the afternoon free to prepare for the debate at night. I spoke morning and afternoon. A large crowd attended both day and night sessions. J. T. was well prepared for the debate. They had a ten minute interrogation of each other after each speech and that proved to be interesting. There was no place to go and hide from having to answer direct questions. Not only did the oral debate do much good (several preachers abandoned the liberals and took their stand), but *Searching The Scriptures* published the debate. Hundreds of the printed debates were circulated throughout the Philippines with the result that the institutional forces were greatly diminished. Twelve were baptized during the day lectures (147 total for the month of work there).

Some of the brethren in Manila had been working with leaders of a Chris-

Kawit, Pagadian City, Mindanao (1975). Connie and Cecil Willis were guest speakers.

tian Church in the Makati area of the city. They had already broken ties with the inter-congregational machinery and had changed the name on their sign to read Dian Street Church of Christ. But they still had a choir and used instrumental music. We spent a Sunday afternoon with the elders and the deacons of that church. We had a good study and were invited to speak the next night at Dian Street. I spoke first on "How to Establish Bible Authority" and then J. T. applied these principles to the issue of instrumental music in worship. We had a long question and answer session and then left. The elders remained until every member was satisfied as to what needed to be done. They sent for us the next afternoon to come and witness the removal of their organ from the premises. Cecil Willis and I spoke in that very building in 1975; in fact, we had a three day lecture program there. I am sorry to say that the preacher of that group went into Unitarianism and destroyed that work.

In 1975, Cecil Willis and I journeyed together to the Philippines. While some of that trip has been dealt with in an earlier chapter, it is noteworthy that a total of 128 were baptized on that trip. After Cecil suffered a stroke in Mindanao, I left him with some of the brethren in Manila and several brethren accompanied me to Tablas on the island of Romblon. I was the first American brother to preach there, though brother Menor, from Calapan, Mindoro and Victorio Tibayan, from Manila, had done some work there with the small congregation established mainly through their efforts. They arranged for three days of lectures in a school. For the first and only time in my work as a preacher, there was a public ceremony to welcome us there. The mayor spoke and expressed their gratitude for my coming and wished us well in our lectures. He attended some of the lectures and showed much interest and then, the last night, asked for the floor at the conclusion of our meeting, to thank me again for coming. We baptized two policemen that week, and the driver of our jeepney.

Among the twenty-nine who were baptized during that meeting, there was a denominational preacher and wife who obeyed the gospel the first day. He was financially supported and provided a house and some fringe benefits. I asked him what would happen when his overseers found out what he had done. He said, "They kick me out." Well, the last day, he came to me and said, "They find out." They gave him one week to vacate the house and, of course, his salary was immediately terminated. I asked what he planned to do. He said, "My wife and nine children are going to live in the house of my cousin (in a town 30 km away, CWA), for six months while I go home with brother Menor to Calapan, Mindoro and study the Bible with him." That is exactly what he did. Brother Menor had daily studies with him; he made a few trips to Romblon on weekends to see his family (with fare provided by brother Menor) and then moved back there, converted his relatives and some others. He then established a second congregation at the other end of town. He worked in the fields, and drove a jeepney to provide for his family. I relate this because some have questioned the genuineness of the conversion of some in the Philippines. Could twenty-nine people be truly converted in three days? In the first place, teaching had taken place already. These people would be converted whether an American were present or not. But I have to ask this and I wish somebody would give me a decent answer. How could 3,000 be baptized on Pentecost? Were they really taught? Did they really mean it, or were they just emotionally excited?

I did not return to the Philippines again until 1999. In the intervening twenty-four years, much work had been done, thousands had been converted and hundreds of congregations had been established. We found some churches of substantial size fully organized with elders and deacons. In the cities, we saw evidence, in some homes of Christians, of material improvement. But for the most part, even in the larger cities, most of the brethren are very poor. In the Davao and General Santos City areas on Mindanao, there are hundreds of brethren who are evacuees from war ravaged areas caused by rebel insurgents who are in military conflict with the government. They are living in tents, many are hungry, some have actually starved, there is much disease, and the end of their troubles seems to be nowhere in sight. In 2002 when we made our last trip, I met with over 100 preachers from the mountainous region of what are called "minority tribes" to hear them tell of their work amid unbelievable trials. A number of them looked gaunt and undernourished.

Bobby went with me in 1999 and 2002 to teach classes for women in many places. For years, brethren pleaded with American preachers who visited, to bring their wives to teach and train their women how to teach children and how to conduct themselves as godly women. Her classes ranged in attendance from 25-30 to 300 at several places and over 500 at Allisitan, Pamplona in the Cagayan Valley, Luzon. These women were hungry to hear the word from an older sister in Christ. While I taught the men in the meeting house or in a side yard to a house, the brethren would cover a large area with canvass for the women. I told Bobby that, if she started having more women to teach than I had men to instruct, she could not go with me any more. You can't have your wife upstaging you, can you? Well, that happened at several places and I had to back down.

Living conditions in many places there are far more primitive than we are accustomed to in our country. Often, you have to shower by pouring a bucket of cold water over you, soaping up, and then pouring another bucket of cold water over you to rinse. Bathroom facilities are, well, let's just say they are different and leave much to be desired. Bobby and I both grew up in the country and were familiar with outhouses and we managed. But differences in food and conveniences are small when you see the eagerness of people to hear the gospel taught. In most places there we would have as much preaching in one day as we Americans would have in a week. I have seen people who walked long distances, sit on benches with no backs and with their feet on the ground instead of a floor. Add to all of this, the fact that most classes or sermons have to be interpreted, so everything must be said twice. But still they come and listen by the hour. The usual meeting will begin at 8 A.M. with a different speaker each hour. At the end of each speech, they will stand and sing a song and then sit down for another speech. That continues until noon. Then there is a break until about 1:30 P.M. when you usually have two more speeches followed by an open forum. Then after a break for dinner, the evening sessions usually last until 10 P.M. There are times when you can only remain at a place for one service, then travel over rough roads to get to the next place. It is physically and emotionally draining. But it is wonderful. When you stand before eager faces, ready to hear the word, you soon forget how little sleep you had, how tired you are, or how much you would like to have a good shower with warm water. Jesus told the Twelve, "I have meat to eat that ye know not of." I am convinced He had something like this in mind.

In 1999 when we flew into Cagayan de Oro City on the north shore of Mindanao, we were met by Edgar Samodal from Illigan City with his truck, made into a jeepney. We were also greeted by Ramon Carino and his dear wife who were to accompany us for the five hour trip to Pagadian City for three days of preaching. They insisted that Bobby and I ride in the front with Edgar. The rest rode in the back which had a top and benches on either side the length of the truck bed. I thought the Carinos should have the front, but they would not hear of it. Edgar seemed to be in a great hurry. While it was unspoken, I knew the reason. He wanted to get us to Pagadian City before dark, if at all possible, for we were to travel through Muslim territory. He did not slow up much even through villages and towns with people very close to the edge of the road. Bobby asked him what the speed limit was. He replied, "However fast it will run." His speedometer was broken but we knew we were moving on by how quickly the coconut palms were running together. We did not arrive before dark and he became very quiet and watchful until we arrived at the meeting house in Pagadian City where we found a large banner welcoming us, and with our names printed in large letters along with the dates of the meeting. There was a large turnout of brethren who had been waiting for us for several hours. We were warmly greeted, adorned with beautiful leis of tropical flowers and made to feel very special. There was a brief service in which brother Carino made some very gracious remarks and asked me to say a few words. We were bone tired, but there was something exhilarating about it all. I have described this reception (it was typical of many others we received) because I have been embarrassed when we have had a few brethren visit here from the Philippines or some other country to be received with so little appreciation, and reluctance to even allow them time enough to speak to us about the work they are doing, or even to have time just to thank us for whatever part we may have in it. Embarrassed is not the right word. I have been ashamed when I recall how special they have made us feel.

Back to Edgar. He is a fine preacher. The day we were to leave Pagadian City to retrace our route to Cagayan de Oro City, I told the brethren I was renaming him. I would henceforth call him "Jehu, for he driveth furiously." Well, that name stuck. After we returned home, when he wrote to us, he signed his letters, Jehu. When their son was born later, they named him Jehu. Now when I hear from Edgar, he signs his letters, Jehu, Sr.

There are a number of children in the Philippines who are named for some of the Americans who have gone there to preach. There is Hafley Caa and Dudley Balbin. We have two who are named to honor us. Juanito Balbin's youngest son is named W. Connie Balbin. I had the privilege of baptizing him in 2002 and now he is preaching while he completes his schooling. Julie Notarte's wife was expecting a new arrival at any time when we were at Digos in Mindanao. A few days after we left, a son was born whom they named Connie Bobby. They call him C. B. Three of these namesakes are already preaching the gospel. In fact, many of the Filipino preachers have trained their sons to preach.

Brethren in the Philippines have many problems. There have been some unworthy men who have sought and received financial support until their evils have been exposed. But you know, that is not the only place where there have been some unworthy brethren. One of the Twelve betrayed the Lord. Another one denied Him. Others vied for seats of honor in the kingdom. Demas forsook Paul and, apparently, the Lord. There were false teachers, and even elders who fell away. Among believers the world over, there will be some who love the world, or are hypocritical, or espouse false doctrine. Some of the troubles suffered by brethren there were exported from the USA. Thankfully, there are a number of older, mature brethren there who have been able to help work through many issues which have confronted the churches. I have worked in several countries and it is my conviction that the Philippines remain one of the most fertile fields for sowing the seed of the kingdom in all the world.

The Gospel in Italy

After World War II, Italy was targeted by some brethren to preach the gospel and establish churches. Cline Paden and several others were sent, being sponsored by the church in Brownfield, Texas. They converted a number of people but soon encountered the wrath of the Catholic Church. There were many unpleasant incidents in which services were interrupted by angry mobs, rocks were thrown at some leaving a baptismal scene near the pope's summer home. A legal battle ensued over the right to post a sign advertising a meeting place of the church. One of the conditions of surrender at the end of the war was the guarantee of religious freedom. The brethren prevailed in court and in time the persecution subsided. But they established more than congregations. They built Frascati Orphan home, the Florence Bible School, and Bible camps. A bond developed between the churches and these institutions. Further, as the first wave of preachers came home, their replacements were not as firm in their teaching. With every set of replacements, the weakening continued.

In 1974, as editor of *Searching The Scriptures*, I received an article entitled "From Italy With Sadness." It was co-authored by Rodolfo Berdini and Allesandro Corazza. It told of a downward spiral in the work there from the earlier days. I did not know these men and hesitated to print their article without further information. James W. Adams had said something about a contact with a brother Buta in Sicily. The Pruett and Lobit church in Baytown, Texas had supported him for awhile and he had visited them on at least one occasion. Brother Adams remembered hearing brother Buta mention the names of these two men. It turns out that they were the first two men to be converted in Italy after the war. Corazza was the first, and then Berdini the next. I decided to correspond with them to learn more about them. Brother Corazza was preaching for the Via Sannio church in Rome and was receiving support from a church in Texas. He was engaged in translating into Italian a significant number of books to be used by brethren there. One of the first was *The New Testament Church* by Roy Cogdill. Rodolfo Berdini was preaching at Aprilia, the largest congregation in Italy. He was an eloquent and forceful preacher. Both of these men became disillusioned by the doctrinal softness of the continuing replacements in the work and by the efforts at control by the supporting churches in the USA. Each of them wrote to the churches supporting them and refused to any longer receive their financial fellowship since it was obvious, to them, that they were not standing on the same ground. The liberal brethren thought that if they ignored them, their work would fold without American support. Sandro Corazza took a job with the Italian government as a mine inspector and he and the brethren at Via Sannio mortgaged their homes to secure the building for the church. The liberals' effort failed and the church continues to this day meeting in that property not far from the old Appian Way. Rodolfo Berdini became a building architect and designer. I saw several elegant buildings which he designed. He also continued to preach at Aprilia. For awhile these men did not know of American brethren who had suffered from the same malady which had afflicted the Italian work. Brother Glenn Jones, who was working in Germany, made contact with these men and gave them some periodicals, such as *Truth Magazine, The Preceptor,* and *Searcing The Scriptures.* The article detailing the apostate practices was sent to each of these papers. The editors of the other two papers had the same reservations I did and chose not to print the article. But after I corresponded with these men, it was evident to me what the situation was and I asked them what we could do to help. They replied that, if "help" meant we wanted to come and dominate the churches there and try to keep them under American control, then they said, "No thank you, Sir, we have already experienced that." I assured them that no such intentions existed, but there were scriptural issues at stake and, if we could study with them and help with scriptural cooperation, we were ready to come and talk with them. They talked to brethren in Rome, Aprilia, and at Poggiomarino, near Naples and they seemed eager for some of us to come. In the meantime, I did print the article and it caused a firestorm among the liberals. The Italian institutional folks, who had ignored them for years, came to see each of them. They told Corazza and Berdini what bad people we "antis" were. Brother Corazza asked them, "Are they against you?" "Oh yes," they replied. Then he said, "Well, thank the Lord for them, so are we."

I had already committed to go with Cecil Willis to the Philippines in the spring of 1975, but knew someone needed to go right away. James W. Adams and Roy Cogdill planned to go until brother Cogdill had some health problems which made it impossible for him to go. So, Foy Vinson agreed to go with James W. Adams. They were graciously received and had many productive studies with brethren there. In 1976, H. E. Phillips and I did go and spend almost a month preaching and teaching in Rome, Aprilia, Pomezia, and Poggiomarino. We were warmly received. Both of Corazza's sons, Arrigo and Stefano, came to Florida College as did two of the children of Rodolfo Berdini, Gianni and Antonella. The Berdini's older daughter, Rosanna, was already married to a very capable preacher, Roberto Tondelli, who preaches for the church in Pomezia. Gianni Berdini and Stefano Corazza boarded with H. E. and Polly Phillips while they were in Tampa. While students there, Stefano and Antonella discovered each other and married. The younger generation is hard at work in Italy. Stefano works with his aged father in Rome. Gianni and his family work with the church at Trieste in northeastern Italy. My first Bobbie and I made a trip to Italy to visit among the brethren, and Bobby 2 and I have been twice since. All of these Italian brethren have been in our home and we hold them in fond affection and memory. While he was working in Udine, Stefano converted a very capable young lawyer and professor, Valerio Marchi, who still works with the church in Udine. We have been there twice for meetings. I asked Sandro Corazza once what we could do to help them the most. He replied, "Pray for a severe persecution. That is when we will grow the most." When he took an early retirement from his work with the government, he used his funds to purchase a print shop for the express purpose of printing material to be used for years to come by brethren in Italy. He has translated into Italian many books, including those of Robert Harkrider, *Salmon's Infallibility*, *Catholicism Against Itself* (two volumes) by O.C. Lambert, the *Campbell-Purcell Debate*, the entire *Truth in Life* literature series, and all but the most recent *Truth Commentaries*.

Before H. E. Phillips and I boarded our plane for Rome, at Kennedy Airport in New York, we found a quiet place where we could pray together. For some

Church in Badalona, Spain (1993)

reason that moment stands out as a highlight among my memories. Godly men, like H. E. (we called him Elwood) Phillips, know how to pray and to make their prayers fit the needs of the hour. This was his first trip overseas to preach. After we boarded, I said, "Elwood, you will never be the same after this trip." When we departed from Rome, about thirty brethren came to say goodbye, brethren we had never seen until a month before. When we were seated on the plane and had dried our eyes, he said, "You were right; I'll never be the same again."

Spain and Switzerland

While working with the church at Manslick Road, we had an opportunity to go and preach in Barcelona, Spain. The church at Manslick Road was supporting Efrain Perez in that work. We had met him when he attended the preacher training program which the church at Danville, Kentucky conducted for many years. It was a two year program and Efrain conducted a similar work in Barcelona in which several Spanish men were trained to preach. I conducted a week long meeting and taught daily in their training program in which they had eight men enrolled. Bobby taught some classes for women, using an interpreter.

A year or so later, through contacts from Barcelona, a work was begun in Geneva, Switzerland. Relatives of members in Barcelona formed the nucleus and since they all spoke Spanish, Efrain met us in Geneva and we worked together in the meetings. When I spoke, he interpreted for me. There were also some Americans and some from eastern France who met with us. Geneva was the longtime home of John Calvin. We visited the building where he preached. How many souls have been led astray by the false tenets of Calvinism, only eternity will reveal.

Ramstein, Germany

We have worked twice in meetings with the church which meets near Ramstein, which is a huge U.S. military base. Most of the congregation consists of military families. Some of these are strong workers when they come there, while others are weak and have to be nurtured. Steve and Mary Wallace worked there for many years. Mary was a civil service employee at the base and served as librarian. Steve was not only able to work with the church at Ramstein, but also to reach out to Lithuania and other places in Eastern Europe. At this writing, they have returned to the States.

London, England

On our way home from meetings in Italy, Bobbie 1 and I spent a few days in London. In addition to seeing some of the sights, we were able to worship with what was then called the South London church. They met in a rented community recreational building near the London Tabernacle where the famous Baptist preacher, Charles H. Spurgeon, preached for many years. I preached for the South London church that day. We spent the afternoon in the home of C. T. Jones who was assigned to London in his work. Visiting there that day was a brother from West Africa who had a most interesting story to tell. He had lost his sight, but a surgical procedure in London has restored it. While he was blind, he learned and obeyed the gospel. His comment was, "I had to lose my sight in order to truly see."

I had forgotten to tell Bobbie that most of the English churches used one container for the fruit of the vine. We came into the assembly room after class, and she spotted the large container which had a spread over it. She looked at me and said, "I'm sitting on the front row." Well, she did. They started at the back and she was the last one (out of about sixty) to be served the cup. Be careful what you ask for!

South Africa

We were invited to spend a month working in South Africa in 1998. While it was winter time in the USA it was summer there. Our flight from New York to Johannesburg was the longest one we had ever experienced, something like sixteen hours nonstop. It was also turbulent at times. We connected for a flight into Durban, on the Indian Ocean, where we were met by Paul and Helen Wil-

Church building in Eshowe, South Africa (1998).

liams. After stopping to eat at a Kentucky Fried Chicken place, we drove on to Eshowe where they lived and worked. Eshowe is a small town but has served well as a base of work for the Williames who have spent many years working in that country. It is a diverse, beautiful land. In the highlands toward Johannesburg, you see wheat and corn fields. The terrain reminds me of western Kansas. Johannesburg itself is higher in elevation than Denver, Colorado. The country is rich in natural resources. But it is also crime ridden. We were not in a house which did not have bars on the windows. One preacher has had two cars stolen from his yard. The Williames have had their home broken into. You could not purchase car insurance unless you had an anti-theft device on the vehicle.

The church in Eshowe, at the time we were there consisted of forty to fifty people. The singing was so beautiful it is hard to describe. The harmony is natural but does not follow the musical patterns we are accustomed to hearing. A preacher training program had been planned for two weeks. In addition to preaching three times on Sunday, I taught five classes on "Premillennialism," five classes on "Rightly Dividing the Word," four sessions on "The Preacher and His Work," five lessons on "Institutionalism" and four classes on "Divorce and Remarriage." We had brethren in attendance from Port Elizabeth, Durban, Johannesburg, and a couple of other places,. Scott Tope, Paul Williams, Robert Buch-

Men's class in Eshowe, South Africa (1998).

anan, and Basil Cass also taught along with one other brother. On the weekend, we were driven down to Durban where I preached at three congregations.

One afternoon while I was teaching, there was a terrible commotion up on the tin roof. Paul saw I was startled and he said, "It's all right. They are just baboons fighting." They soon jumped down and chased each other across the road.

When we completed our work at Eshowe on Friday, we were driven by Robert Buchanan up to the northeastern region of the country (through the Transvaal) to his home. The plan was to preach there on Sunday and then rendezvous with the Williames and a brother from Johannesburg and spend most of a week working in Zimbabwe in tribal villages. Then we were to complete our month speaking at Pretoria and in Johannesburg. But our plans had to be altered. After arriving at the home of Robert Buchanan, we received an email from Harold Byers in Louisville that Bobby's mother, who was ninety, had suffered a heart attack. From the tone of his message, we knew it was serious. So, we had to immediately start making plans to get back to Louisville. South African Airways was very cooperative about changing our tickets. Robert Buchanan drove us the four hours to Johannesburg airport. While waiting there, we called the hospital in Louisville and a nurse told us that Bobby's mother was a little better and was sitting up to eat a little. That eased our minds somewhat.

Pinetown church in Durban, South Africa (1998).

Our flight back was long and tiresome. We had to land in the Verde Islands to refuel before flying on to New York. When we arrived in Louisville, we were met by one of our sons, an elder from Manslick Road, and by Bobby's brother and sister-in-law. I took one look at them and knew what was coming. Bobby's mother had passed away while we were somewhere over the Atlantic trying to get home. It was a great shock and Bobby had a hard time with the fact that she was never able to say goodbye. Elsie Shull was a devout woman who loved the Lord with all her heart and who served Him for many years. The day before she went to the hospital, she went with Greg Litmer, the preacher then at Expressway, to visit someone in a nursing home. The best laid plans sometimes have to be changed. But I am thankful that we had that one opportunity to have some part in the work of the gospel in South Africa.

It is a long way from the nine foot road in Newport, North Carolina to the Philippines, and longer still to South Africa. As a boy growing up in Virginia, I never dreamed of having so many doors opened to preach the gospel. I am thankful to my God for making all of that possible. I still believe that "into all the world" means exactly that: into all the world.

Chapter 12

In Journeyings Often

Luther Blackmon once told me that when he was in full time gospel meeting work, along about October each year he wanted to set his suitcase in the floor and kick it. I did not know what he meant until a few years later. During my teen years, our family took the *Gospel Advocate* and I always read the "News and Notes" with interest. As I read accounts of various preachers who conducted gospel meetings in different places across the country, I wondered what it would be like to travel to so many places and experience the things about which those men wrote. It sounded interesting and exciting. That first meeting in 1950 on the nine foot road was only a foretaste of what was to come in the fifty-nine years which have followed so far. Echoes from that meeting have sounded in forty of our states and in fifteen countries. I have packed and unpacked my suitcase so many times I can almost do it in the dark. I have slept on beds, good and bad, in elegant homes, in nipa huts and under mosquito nets. I have fared sumptuously and sparingly. I have driven long hours over familiar and unfamiliar territory in all kinds of weather. I have stayed in hotels and motels, both well furnished and otherwise. Many hours have been spent on buses, or trains (in Europe) and in airports and on planes. I have picked cotton, babysat, washed dishes, worked in yards and gardens, shelled peas, shucked corn, run sweepers, shoveled snow, and otherwise tried to be helpful to good folks who shared with me the best they had. We have crossed rivers, seas, oceans, mountains, deserts, and whole continents to get to some place which opened a door for us to come and preach the gospel.

And yet, when I think of what Paul wrote about his experiences in 2 Corinthians 11:23-33, I am ashamed to either boast or complain. While he traveled by ship and often walked great distances, he never rode in an automobile, bus, train, or plane. He never knew the comfort of an air conditioned room. Sometimes his bedroom was under the stars in mountains where it was freezing cold and without adequate covering. He was beaten, stoned, imprisoned and in grave danger from angry mobs or wild beasts. He never owned a typewriter, cell phone, or computer. Sometimes he was well supported while at other times he was not. He wrote, "I know both how to be abased, and I know how to abound: every where and in all things I am instructed both to be full and to be hungry, both to abound and to suffer need" (Phil. 4:12). Then, when we consider what Jesus did for all of us, suffering even the death on the cross, then our own trials seem as nothing.

In fact, for the most part, brethren have treated me far better than I deserved. They have shared their homes and the bounty of their tables. Even the very poorest have offered the best they had. Once I had dinner with a family in Florida which lived in a rough shack at the end of a sand road, not far from the city dump. The family sat on benches on each side of the table and they gave me *the* chair, the only one they had. I have been paid far more than I expected from very small groups, and very little from large and prosperous places. There have been times when I was paid nothing, and numerous times when I did not break even when all expenses were paid. But I would do it all again, and gladly. It is an honor and a privilege to preach the gospel. Paul called it a "grace." He wrote "Unto me, who am less than the least of all saints, is this grace given, that I should preach among the Gentiles the unsearchable riches of Christ" (Eph. 3:8). "Yea, woe is unto me, if I preach not the gospel" (1 Cor. 9:16).

I doubt that anyone fully understands the churning emotions which compel a man to preach, unless it would be another preacher. As supportive as a man's wife, his children, or his brethren may be, they do not really know the sense of urgency and satisfaction which comes from being able to stand before an audience with an open Bible and proclaim God's truth. Eternal destinies hang in the balance, including that of the preacher himself. Sometimes it is hard to balance that compulsion against the demands of family life. I have missed birthdays and anniversaries and other special events, sometimes being in far away places with my mind torn between what I was missing (and what my family missed by my absence) and the sense of duty that brought me to that place. I tried to make it up the best I could. But sometimes it nearly tore me apart. I have seen preachers lose their own while trying to save everyone else. I was blessed in having a godly wife (two of them) who knew how to keep the home fires burning, discipline the children when they needed it, and give me the support needed to continue in the work to which I committed my life years before. If they ever whined, they did not let me know.

Once, when I was away in a meeting, an older sister was sympathizing with my first Bobbie. She said, "Is brother Adams gone again? How do you stand it?" Without missing a beat (and with a twinkle in her eye), she replied, "Why that's when I put on my blond wig and go to town and have a big time." The dear lady never offered her sympathy again. It was Bobbie who encouraged me to go again to the Philippines in 1975. She had read some of the letters I received from brethren there and came to feel as if she knew them.

My second Bobby has traveled with me to at least 400 meetings. When we married, all the children were grown and on their own. We have had much togetherness and it has been wonderful. We never seem to run out of something to talk about. She is an excellent traveler. We share the driving (when we travel by car). When I drive, she reads the Bible aloud early in the morning and has cross stitched many special things for grandchildren when they marry or for new arrivals in the family. Sometimes we just watch the passing scenery as we listen to music or to talk radio. We stop about every two hours and walk for ten or fifteen minutes. Once, after I had back surgery and could only sit for twenty minutes at a time, we drove to California for two meetings and then on to Oregon for two more. I made a bed in the back seat and she did most of the driving. I read, studied the clouds out of the rear window, or listened to music. About every two hours, after we stopped to walk, I would drive for twenty minutes to give her a little break, then stop and return to my bed in the back seat. I could stand or walk, but sitting was a problem. But we managed very well and kept our appointments.

We did have one anxious experience on that trip. We were in a canyon on I-70 a few miles east of Glenwood Springs, Colorado when the road narrowed to two lanes and then all traffic was stopped both ways for about 45 minutes for some blasting to widen the highway. Traffic was backed up for quite some distance in both directions. I had been taking one of my twenty minute turns when we were stopped. We decided that would be a good time to stretch our legs. I had no more than closed the door when I realized I had left the keys in the ignition. Usually, when we stopped to walk, Bobby took her keys with her. Not that time! She had two sets of keys in her purse, locked in the car and mine dangled from the ignition. Truckers right behind us tried to help and then urged us to just break a glass to get in the car. We did not want to do that. The lady who flagged us down called a locksmith in Glenwood Springs and that would take about thirty minutes. The truckers were anxious. There was no way for them to pass us and we were at the head of the line of traffic. A highway patrolman made his way to us along the shoulder of the road and tried to open the door with a "slim Jim" which succeeded in breaking the lock on the passenger side. Finally, he decided to try once on the driver's side and it worked the first try. About two minutes later, they turned the traffic loose in both directions. I don't want to think about dealing with those truckers while waiting for that locksmith!

We have been privileged to see many interesting places on our way to a meeting or in returning from one. We would never have seen these places otherwise. Our travels have never been boring to us. Whether it was the desert southwest, the badlands of South Dakota, the rockbound coast of Maine, the Smoky Mountains, the Gulf Coast of Florida, the Grand Canyon, the Rocky Mountains, or the Pacific Coast of California, Oregon, and Washington, our eyes have beheld the wonders of God's creation. We had a meeting in Geneva, Switzerland followed by one in Bergen, Norway. We bought a Eurail pass and rode on thirteen different trains to get to Bergen. One time after several meetings in Italy, we took a train from Trieste through Austria and spent two delightful days in Salzburg where we took the "Sound of Music" tour and took a cable car up to a mountain overlooking the city where we heard a Mozart concert in a castle that was 1,000 years old. We have stood in somber reflection in the American military cemetery at Anzio in Italy and thought of the price of freedom. We have met brethren of many languages and different races and have been brought face to face with the truth Peter expressed when he said, "but in every nation he that feareth him, and worketh righteousness, is accepted with him" (Acts 10:35). I told Bobby that if she would marry me, we would go places. I am sure she did not realize at the time how literally that would come true.

Why Have Gospel Meetings?

Does all of this serve a useful purpose in God's scheme of things or is it all wasted effort? First of all, a gospel meeting is just what the term implies: it is a series of gatherings in which the gospel is preached. "How beautiful are the feet of them that preach the gospel of peace, and bring glad tidings of good things" (Rom. 10:15). Since the gospel is "the power of God unto salvation" (Rom. 1:16), then that message must be preached. All will not receive it. They did not all receive it when it first fell from the lips of inspired men. But all men have a right to hear it. If they receive it, they will be saved. If they do not, they will be lost in the sins which separated them from God. They were offered the divine remedy and refused it. Whether the message is accepted or rejected, the messenger has served his purpose.

We need to be sure that the message delivered is indeed the gospel and not some cheap substitute. I fear that some meetings offer more or far less than the gospel. Paul said to Timothy, "Preach the word" (2 Tim. 4:2). That word is "quick and powerful" (Heb. 4:12). It pricks the hearts of sinners (Acts 2:37). It moves them to repentance and obedience in baptism. It exhorts, reproves, and rebukes the hearers and challenges them to grow in the grace and knowledge of Christ (2 Tim 4:2-4; 2 Pet. 3:18). Entertaining performances with snappy one-liners, leg slapping humor, or sob stories do not constitute preaching the word. Preaching does not have to be dry or dull. Humor and tears are natural ingredients of life. But men who go out to preach need to consider what their task really is. Paul said he was not a "man pleaser" (1 Thess. 2:4) and that, if he sought to please men, he "should not be the servant of Christ" (Gal. 1:10). I heard it said of one preacher, "He is a great preacher. He is hilarious." I wonder if the preaching of Christ, Peter, Paul, James, John or Timothy was ever described that way?

There are basic subjects which need to be preached. Sermons should be preached on such subjects as divine authority, the deity of Christ, the cross, the resurrection, the church, the law and the gospel, the plan of salvation, the nature, work, organization and worship of the church, exposing of various errors which confront God's people at a given time and place, godly living, heaven, hell, expositions of various books of the Bible, and the list goes on. There is never any excuse for preachers to run out of something to preach. Men need to spend less time reading after or listening to Rick Warren, Billy or Frank Graham, Chuck Swindol, Max Lucado, or Zig Ziglar, and more time with the prophets, our Lord, and His apostles. That would be far more rewarding to them and to their hearers.

Over the years, as I have preached in meetings across this country, I have looked at bulletin boards announcing area meetings. It is refreshing to see real gospel subjects announced and equally depressing to see such subjects as "Who Ate Paul's Cheese?," or "The Wizard of Oz," or "Seven Ducks in Muddy Water," or other such sensational topics. This reduces the gospel to the realm of the theatre marquee with its eye catching subjects for entertainment. I have heard some men speak for thirty minutes and never read or quote a verse of Scripture. They have had the audience rolling in laughter or shedding tears, but the old Jerusalem gospel was nowhere to be seen or heard.

Real gospel meetings serve a number of useful purposes. There should always be a desire to convert the lost and to edify the saved. I have had meetings in which I was asked to preach on first principles with the promise that they would work hard to bring lost people to hear. In a meeting at Hueytown, Alabama I was asked to preach the whole meeting on conversion, using a different case of conversion from Acts each night. There are meetings to address special needs in a congregation or in the general area. Sometimes meetings are planned to help godly families with the challenges they face in a changing culture. In many meetings where we have had day services in addition to evening gatherings, I have preached expository sermons through books of the Bible. My own preference in a meeting is to cover a number of bases. I still believe it is necessary to try to reach the lost, including the children of the members. It does not hurt those who have been faithful for years to hear sermons on the fundamentals of the gospel. "I love to tell the story, for those who know it best, seem hungering and thirsting, to hear it like the rest." It does not hurt non-Christians to hear sermons dealing with issues facing the church. During the 1950's and 1960's when we had to deal with institutional issues, my records show that we continued to baptize people in those very meetings.

Some General Observations

How long should a meeting last? There is a trend in recent years to make them shorter and shorter. I call them bob-tailed meetings. Some churches have opted for weekend meetings only. There may be a place for such abbreviated meetings to deal with specific needs of a congregation. Some churches will have a Sunday-Wednesday or Sunday-Tuesday meeting and that is all they ever have. My records of meetings since 1950 show that the longer meetings have been the most productive in terms of the number who responded to the gospel. Of course, that is not the only measure of success. Whenever the truth is taught then good is done, whether or not we see immediate results. But it appears to me that many have given up on trying to convert people during meetings. The first meeting, on the nine foot road, was a two Sunday effort. Later that same year I had a meeting which covered three Sundays. The generation before me had even longer meetings which resulted in many conversions and in the establishment of many congregations. Two week meetings gave way to ten or eleven days. While living in Akron and working in the two preacher arrangement, we had a number of ten day meetings. Usually the attendance would build from Monday and we would begin having responses to the gospel call on Sunday and then each service right to the end. By the time we moved to Louisville, most congregations had opted for six or seven day meetings. The pattern then became Sunday-Friday meetings and most of mine to this day fall into that category. If one of our objectives is to convert people to Christ, it takes time to lay a foundation near the beginning of the week, and then move to motivational material toward the end to move people to obedience. There is also something to be said for time for the truth to marinate from one night to the next. With the Sunday-Friday meetings, we usually begin with motivational material on Sunday, then have to backtrack to fundamentals for the first part of the week and then you run out of time before you can have sermons to persuade those you have taught the basics earlier. Much meeting preaching is almost entirely motivational. There is surely a place for some of that. But people must first be instructed in the truth of the gospel before they are persuaded to act. Otherwise, any response is likely to be emotional and short lived.

One large congregation in my acquaintance decided to try a two week's meeting and see how it would go. The crowd grew every night from the first to the last. The first week, none responded to the invitation. But then, the second week, several were baptized and others restored who had been unfaithful. It worked. But you know what? They never tried it again and have settled for Sunday-Wednesday meetings only. Go figure.

It is difficult for preachers who spend most of their time in meetings to schedule them to the satisfaction of all concerned. In the spring, there is Easter and spring break (and that is different from place to place). Then you have to work around Memorial Day, the fourth of July, Labor Day, and Thanksgiving. Nobody wants to plan a meeting involving a Sunday just before or right after those times. In the fall, there are football rivalries to be avoided. I have had meetings in which we had very good attendance and interest until that Friday night when many of the young people, as well as their parents, were absent. The football game trumped the gospel meeting. And then we wonder why we can't convert some of the young people. All of this has raised a pertinent question: When are we going to preach the gospel so it will not inconvenience anyone?

Sometimes, people ask me, "Why don't we have meetings like we used to have?" There are several reasons for that. Times have changed and many are not nearly as interested in spiritual things as former generations were. There are many distractions and too many do not have their priorities in order. Another difference is the fact that gospel meetings are no longer regarded as special events. They are looked upon as optional occasions. It is nice to attend unless we have something else which we think is far more important. How refreshing it is to find a few brethren who actually take vacation time so they won't have to miss any of a gospel meeting. I had one meeting in California during which two of the elders took a vacation to the beach and took some other families with them. They were also the same ones who taught the young people that a one piece swim suit was modest at the beach, but a bikini might be immodest. Most congregations post the dates of planned meetings far in advance, yet there are members who will take off and claim that they had reservations for over a month, when the meeting had been scheduled for anywhere from two to five years with the dates posted on the bulletin board. Children are overloaded with extra curricular activities from scouting to little league baseball, or soccer, or Pop Warner football and these take precedence over gospel meetings. I have preached in many meetings where the house would be full to overflowing every service and I have also preached in meetings where the home folks just would not attend. If not for the presence of brethren from other places, who had more interest than the local members, it would have been embarrassing. When meetings are treated again as special events for which other things are put aside, then you will see a great difference, even with all the cultural changes we are experiencing.

Another reason meetings are not as effective as they once were is the way singing is treated. In the generation before me, as well as in meetings in the earlier part of my preaching work, very often brethren would invite a visiting song leader along with the visiting preacher, often when they had adequate song leaders in the congregation. This added another special ingredient. Sometimes singing instruction would be given before the evening services would begin and new songs would be learned. But for some reason, brethren have decided, in many places, to have a different song leader at every service. A few congregations are blessed with a number who do that work well. But all song leaders are not equal. In my own experience, the singing is usually better and the song selection more attuned to the sermon subjects, with the same leader each time. Some congregations who have several very capable leaders, have solved the problem by choosing one to lead for a meeting, then another for the next meeting. I have seen a song leader on Thursday night, for instance, lead the same songs we sang Monday night. You see, he had to work Monday night and did not bother to check with the other leaders. At one meeting in Alabama a brother was called on to lead one night who had *never* led a song before in his life. We had to "break him in" right in the middle of a gospel meeting. Folks, there is a time to learn new songs and to break in would be song leaders, but during a gospel meeting is not the time. The meeting should be a special event and a time to put your best foot forward. It is not a training class. While this

With R.J. Stevens, preacher and song leader for Southside lectures (June, 1984).

is not true of all song leaders, I have noticed a rivalry, bordering on jealousy, among some song leaders. If an inept song leader is to be used "so he won't get his feelings hurt" then he is too immature to take any public part until he grows up and becomes stronger in the faith.

Over the last two decades, I have noticed that we see fewer and fewer young people obeying the gospel. Other preachers and I have agonized over this, have wondered why this was so, and what could be done to change it. Parents who truly care about the souls of their children have many things working against them. In some instances, the public schools are purveyors of secularism and work to undermine the values of godly parents. Some are blissfully ignorant of this and are puzzled at the lack of interest in spiritual things, at defiant behavior, and at being excluded from the world into which their own children have locked themselves. One thing which becomes more apparent all the time is the fact that many of our young people have grown up without hearing the gospel. You may wonder how that can be when they have been taken to every service since infancy. But young parents have gone to services with large bags full of things to amuse their small children—books, toys, and food. Listen, they don't need to eat, unless they are infants and nursing. And you don't have to take *anything* to amuse them. Start at home and teach them reverence during prayers and when the Bible is being read. Impress on them, *at home*, that when they go to worship, they are to sit quietly and listen. When they are old enough to write, show them how to take notes and to copy what is on the board or the PowerPoint charts. Have them to write down each Scripture reference. I have had many children to come to me to show me their notes. Often they attempt to draw my picture and some of them think I have a very long nose and huge ears! But they are listening and learning. When you take distractions with them when they are small, as they grow older they will discover other ways not to listen. I have seen some who are allowed to do their home work, to read a book, or even to play with a game boy. Do you suppose that helps to explain why they don't obey the gospel when they get to be teenagers? Could it be that they have been taught how *not* to listen? Paul said, "So then faith comes by hearing, and hearing by the word of God" (Rom. 10:17).

We have a crop of young parents who do not know what to do with a disruptive child during services. The older generation had no such problem. They did know what to do. Take a child out before he/she completely destroys a prayer, meditations during the Lord's Supper, or some critical point during a sermon that might even affect the eternal destiny of some lost soul who is trying to hear what is being said. If the child is sick, then comfort it. If it needs changing, then take care of that. If the child is just being ornery and challenging your authority, then establish that beyond all doubt. In such cases, you take them out, wear them out, and then bring them back in the assembly. If they persist in unruly conduct, then take them out again, wear them out again, and bring them back into the assembly. Repeat that treatment until the child understands that it is far more pleasant to stay in than to go out! If you can't establish who is in control with a two, three, or four year old, then when they get to be teenagers, you will have grief such as you never knew existed.

Gospel meetings are not status symbols. Many good brethren prefer not to conduct many meetings and to devote their time and attention to their local work. Meetings are blessings to the cause of Christ. When I began preaching, I had no idea I would ever be involved in as many meetings as has been the case over my lifetime. I have never invited myself for a meeting. But it has always been hard for me to turn one down. My practice has been to schedule them on a first-come-first-served basis. I have agreed to go to whatever place asked first for the time I had available, regardless of where it was, the size of the church, or whether they could pay me well or not at all. Since 1975, I have had some underwriting which has provided a stable base of income so we could pay our bills and still accept whatever invitations came. Bobby and I have worked many times with small churches which were struggling and have taken delight in seeing them brighten up and take on new life by the time a meeting would end. Her women's classes have added much even in small congregations. We cherish the friendships which have been formed with some of the best people on earth. This has made our lives rich and full.

As long as men are lost in sin, there will be a need for God's remedy to be prescribed. That remedy is still the gospel. Paul wrote to the Corinthians about the gospel which he preached unto them "by which also ye are saved, if you keep in memory what I preached unto you" (1 Cor. 15:1-4). Some churches are hearing only one sermon a week. That is not enough. Gospel meetings are still needed for the same reasons as before. God has opened many more doors than we ever dreamed possible and we thank him for every one and for those who have made it possible for us to go and do what we could.

Before closing this chapter, I have to tell you about a young sister I met at East Alton, Illinois. It was a Monday night, the first night of a seven-day meeting, and I arrived at the building early. A young woman parked right behind me and started toward the building. She had a large notebook and an oversized Bible. She waited at the door for me and said, "You must be brother Adams." I assured her I was. Then she said, "I'm so excited I can hardly contain myself. I have just been a Christian for a month and this is my first gospel meeting, ever." I thought it would be wonderful if we could somehow bottle that attitude. I have known some brethren who needed a good drink of such an elixir. That surely beats the hangdog, disappointed attitude which says in essence, "Oh no, not another meeting." Yes, we have been in journeyings often, but such eager souls as that young woman have made it all worthwhile, not to mention the encouragement from those dear souls who arrive with canes, walkers, or in wheel chairs.

Chapter 13

A Time To Laugh

The Preacher wrote saying that there is "a time to weep, and a time to laugh." Preaching the gospel is serious work. Those of us who preach are concerned with the salvation of souls so they might be prepared for the judgment. The work is both challenging and rewarding. But there are lighter moments which serve as balm to the spirit, which might otherwise be weighted down with sorrow or anxiety. Every preacher has his own stories to tell, some more than others. Often we have been enjoying the company of hospitable Christians when I would relate something humorous which had occurred in my work, when someone would remark, "You ought to write a book." Well, I guess that is what I am attempting to do. But if you are ever in a group of preachers and they start telling funny stories, you will notice that the first one who tells one does not stand a chance. There will always be someone to top it.

That Reminds Me . . .

James P. Miller was a master at relating humorous incidents. But he was also used to being the star of the show in that department. Once during a meeting at Owensboro, Kentucky he met his match. A. C. Grider was the local preacher. When they were in a social gathering, brother Miller would tell one of his stories and brother Grider would then say, "Now that reminds me. . ." and he would top what Miller had told. In one of his sermons, brother Miller was pointing out the danger of becoming entrapped in human traditions. He told about a sign on the highway, years before, in the days of the T-Model Ford, when roads were often muddy and barely passable. The sign said, "Choose your rut carefully; you'll be in it for the next twenty miles." Later that night they were invited into a home for refreshments when brother Grider said, "That story you told about the rut, reminds me. . . ." He then proceeded to tell about

A. C. Grider (left) and James P. Miller (right)

a man walking down a muddy road when he saw a straw hat in the road. He picked it up, and it was on top of a man's head. He asked him if he was standing on the bottom. The man replied, "No, I'm standing on a load of hay." "Do you want me to get my tractor and pull you out?" He asked. To which the gentleman replied, "No, as soon as I get the cracker fixed on my whip, I think my team of horses can pull me out." Miller said, "That does it! I am never going to hold another meeting where Grider preaches. Every time I tell something he says, 'Now that reminds me . . . and he tops me every time.'"

A Leaky Boat

While Bobbie 1 and I were living in Lake City, Florida in our first local work, Clinton D. Hamilton came to hold a meeting and stayed with us. He was the Dean of Students at Florida Christian College and had held that office while Bobbie and I were students. He had called me on the carpet once, I thought unjustly, and we had some strong words between us. To the day of his

Clinton D. Hamilton (1952)

death, I am sure he wondered if what happened was an effort on my part to get even. We got up early one morning to go fishing in a lake which was on the property of one of the members. He had a boat which sat out in the edge of the lake. I had fished there before in that very boat. It leaked a little, but by setting in the edge of the water, the leaky places were swollen enough that you could manage by bailing the water out now and then. But, this time, there had been a dry spell and the water line had receded so that the boat had parched in the summer Florida sun for several days. We rolled up our britches to our knees and pushed the boat out in the water, intending to fish near some trees which were in the middle of the lake. Brother Hamilton sat down on the back of the boat while I stood at the front with an oar and pushed us out into the water. We had not gone far when I felt the water rising above my ankles. Then I heard a splashing sound. I looked around and brother Hamilton had a syrup bucket and was baling water in both directions. The water kept rising and he was losing the battle. Finally, he said, "Connie, we're going to sink. What should we do?" I suggested that he stand up. He did and the boat went glug, glug, glug, right down to the bottom of that lake. The water was about chest deep at that point. That's when he said, "I can't swim, what are we going to do?" I said, "Well, we are either going to have to stay here or else wade to shore." We stepped out of the boat in long, slimey grass. He said, "What if we step on a snake?" I told him we would have to take our chances. That ended the fishing trip and provided both of us with a good story to tell, though I think his version varied from mine in some details. But then, a story that does not get better with the telling, is not worth telling anyhow. There is a moral to this. Boats belong in the water, but you don't want water in the boat. Apply that to the Christian and the world.

Falling Out of the Pulpit

My brother, Wiley, has had enough unusual things to happen to him to generate a whole series of books. When he was preaching in Fairmont, West Virginia, he was invited to conduct a gospel meeting at Joe's Run, out in the mountains a few miles. Where he preached in Fairmont, the pulpit stand sat back about three feet from the edge of the platform. Wi-

ley had a habit of walking around to the side of the pulpit and then would sometimes step right in front of the stand and lean back against it for awhile as he talked to the people. At Joe's Run, the platform was higher off the floor and the pulpit stand was even with the edge of the platform. He started his first sermon that Monday night and as he began to warm to his subject, he sauntered around to the side of the pulpit stand and then, forgetting where he was, attempted to step in front of the stand. He fell lengthwise across the communion table. The audi-

Wiley Adams (1966)

ence was stunned. He was not hurt, except for his pride.

He scraped himself off the table and then, with what dignity he had left, got back on the platform. He said, "Now, folks, I know it's unusual for you to see the preacher fall out of the pulpit. It is unusual for me. I am not hurt, but it is funny, so let's all have a good laugh about it so I can go on with my sermon." He reared back and was about to have a good laugh, when he realized that every soul present was staring at him with solemn countenance and he was the only one in the house laughing.

Weighty Words

In a meeting at Bruce, Mississippi I did not understand how weighty my words would become. It was a Monday night, the first service of a seven-day meeting. The brethren had a very attractive building, located across the street from the city library. They had remodeled the building some time before and had bricked the exterior. But they failed to vent it properly. It was bricked all the way to the ground. The underpinning was old and, with the humidity, time had taken its toll and the floor joists had rotted. We had the house full that night. I had just closed a meeting the night before at Houston, Mississippi, a few miles away, and many from there had come to encourage us at Bruce. I was almost finished with my sermon on "The Parable of the Sower" when I heard a subdued crunching sound. At first, I did not know what had happened. Then I noticed that two pews were badly slanted toward one side of the house. Both pews were filled and both rows appeared to be leaning. The floor had given way and had fallen in about two feet. This actually involved the area of three pews. Nobody got up and nobody said a word. I hastily ended my sermon and closed the service. The brethren were embarrassed, but I told them that it only proved that my words were "weighty and powerful." I have heard some people say that if they were to go to church "the roof would fall in." But that is the only time I ever knew of the floor falling in.

Cecil and the Parakeet

While we were working in the two-preacher arrangement at Brown Street in Akron, Ohio, Cecil Willis conducted a meeting in Missouri where he stayed with a family which had a pet parakeet. Cecil was annoyed by this bird which had the run of the house. It would fly across the top of his head and leave his hair tangled, or would light on his shoulder and peck his ear lobe. He tried to keep out of the way of what, to him, was a nuisance. One night after service, the family was engrossed in a television program. Cecil was trying to be polite but was totally uninterested in the program. The parakeet flew across the room and landed on a curtain rod a few feet from where Cecil was sitting. One of the boys had a little pistol with a suction stopper. You licked the end of it, pushed it into the pistol and it would stick to the wall or whatever hard surface it struck. Absent mindedly, he pushed that stopper into the pistol and aimed it at the parakeet. Before he realized what he was doing, he pulled the trigger and that stopper made a direct hit on the pet. He watched in horror as the bird fell to the floor right behind a chair. The family had not witnessed this atrocity. While he was trying to figure out how to tell them that he had killed their pet, the bird shook a foot, then his head and then wobbled to his feet and flew across the room. Was that a Freudian shot? At any rate the parakeet gave Cecil a wide berth the rest of the week and he never had to tell the family about it.

The Preacher's Britches

It was July hot in west Tennessee and, take it from me, that is plenty hot. I was holding a seven-day meeting at Fair Haven, out in the country from Lexington, Tennessee. My home that week was with the E. G. Lewises. They lived in a large, two story farm house. It was not air conditioned. My hosts insisted that I take their downstairs bedroom since they said it was the coolest room in the house. They were to sleep upstairs. I felt badly about that, but they insisted. They kept their clothes in a closet under the stairwell, where I also hung mine. One evening, I had supper with them. I got ready early so they could get their clothes out of the room and not have to move things back and forth upstairs. They rode with me to the meeting house that night. We were almost to the building when sister Lewis looked over the back of the seat at her husband who was in the front with me, and said, "E. G., where'd you get them britches?" Then in shock, she said, "Oh my land, you've got on the preacher's britches." I was so tickled I almost had to stop. He sat with a bemused look on his face. She said she was "mortified" and dared me to tell a soul about it. Most of the congregation was related to them and I knew they would enjoy it. I said, "Sister Lewis, that is too good a story to keep to my self. I just have to tell it." And tell it I did. Years later I saw him and asked him if he was still wearing the preacher's britches.

J. T. and the Water Buffalo

On my first trip to the Philippines, along with J. T. Smith, we were met at Ozamis City and had to travel over one hundred miles to Pagadian City where we were to conduct lectures along with several Filipino brethren. Three brethren from Luzon traveled with us down to Mindanao. The road was rough. For about the first hour, we were in a torrential rain. We were traveling in an old Datsun which had seen better days. The windshield wiper did not work. The brakes were bad. It leaked and we all got wet. First gear did not work either, and when we were stopped for some reason, we had to get out and push so the driver could get second gear to catch, then we had to run like crazy to all get in (and in the right sequence). Night fell long before we arrived at our destination. We were in heavily Muslim country and all of us were a little nervous. No, make that a *lot* nervous. Finally we got out of the rain and the moon came up and shone brightly. We met a big truck on a one way wooden bridge and had to back up to let him pass. It was time for the pushing routine. J. T. and I were pushing at the back when I saw a water buffalo tied at the edge of the road. These are domestic animals and are as valuable to a farmer there as a tractor would be to one in Kentucky. J. T. looked around and saw that huge animal not very far from him. He let out a yell and jumped (how high depends on who is telling it). The Filipinos were beside themselves with laughter and teased him about it the rest of the trip. But every time J. T. told it, the horns got longer on that beast. When we were about to board the plane in Manila to start home, one of the brethren who had been with us said, "Tell us again, brother J.T., how long the horns on that water buffalo?" I would give a great deal to have captured his expression on that occasion.

A Boy and His Dog (and My Toothbrush)

In Pensacola, Florida I stayed with a young preacher and his wife during a meeting at Myrtle Grove. I was the first preacher they had kept and the young lady of the house was very nervous about it. I have always tried to make myself at home and be as little trouble as possible when people are kind enough to share their home with me. They had a little boy named David who was a little under the age of two. Just before I arrived, the grandparents had given David a German Shepherd puppy, about eight weeks old. It was obvious that the boy and his dog were fond of each other. It was fun to watch them chase each other through the house or fall down in the floor and wrestle. Toward the end of the week, they were very quiet at breakfast. Finally the wife said, "Jeff, you'll have to tell brother Adams." I could not imagine what had happened. He said, "Brother Adams, you left your toothbrush on the sink in the bathroom last night. When I came into the living room this morning, David had the puppy down in the floor and was brushing his teeth with your toothbrush." He was relieved when I had a big laugh about it, but his wife never did laugh. That made it even funnier to me. I told them that since the puppy had already got used to it, I would just get me another one.

The Shirtless Preacher

Ohio County, Kentucky holds a special place in our hearts. It was at Hopewell in that county where Bobby 2 was born. She graduated from high school at Beaver Dam in the same county. I was preaching in a meeting at Antioch, a community also called "Dog Walk" by some of the locals. But I stayed in Beaver Dam in the home of Lucille Barnes, a gracious sister who was also a very good friend to my mother-in-law to be, Elsie Shull. In one end of the closet where I hung my suits and shirts, were some shirts which had been given to sister Barnes by her son-in-law, Vernon Gary, to be put in a yard sale which she and her daughter-in-law were to have on Saturday of that week. I arose that Saturday morning to the unmistakable smell of bacon frying in the kitchen. I went to the closet to get some jeans and a shirt to wear to breakfast. But when I opened the closet door, there was not one shirt hanging there. I had slept in a tee shirt. I rushed into the kitchen and after saying "Good morning" asked her if she knew what had become of my shirts which were in the closet. She looked stunned for a moment, then put her hand over her mouth and said, "Oh brother Adams, I must have got them mixed up with Vernon's shirts and I have put a price sticker on them for the yard sale and they are all over at Wilna's house hanging in her garage." She called over there to make sure they had not been sold and I went to rescue them. Now, I have heard of preachers not being paid very well for a meeting and saying that they "lost their shirt" on that one, but that is the only time I can truthfully say that I really lost my shirts (plural) in a meeting. While I did manage to retrieve them in time, I still think my shirts were worth a lot more than the amount she was going to ask for them! And before anyone decides that preaching is a good way to get rich, just remember that you could just lose your shirt.

A Sticky, Sweaty Sermon

During the debate and lectures at M'lang, Cotabato on the island of Mindanao in the Philippines in April, 1971, J. T. Smith and I stayed in a small hotel called Foranda's Place. It was run by a man and his wife and two teenaged daughters. It was upstairs over a metal working shop. There were eight small rooms, just large enough for two single beds and with room enough at the end of each bed for a suitcase. Since most Filipinos are short in stature, the beds were short as well. We had to decide whether to let our feet or our heads hang off the end. I opted for my feet hanging off. We had some brethren from Manila with us and others came from Pagadian City, where we had been the week before, to hear the debate. We rented the whole place for $38. That included having our laundry done and breakfast each morning. There was a good sized lounge area where we all gathered at night after the debate, reviewed the events of the evening, and then, as you might expect, traded preacher stories. There was one stall with a commode in it which was to serve all eight rooms. Right out in the hall, near that stall, was a small sink with a cold water tap. We all had to brush our teeth there and also to shave at the sink. Next to the stall with the commode was another stall entered by a door with a very low entrance which struck me just above my eyes. I know that is so because it struck me there twice before I learned to duck. The shower was interesting. It consisted of a half inch pipe bent slightly at the top. There was no nozzle or shower head. The shower was whatever water would run out of that bent pipe. The water supply came from a rain barrel up on top of the building. If it did not rain, there was no water the next day. For two mornings, I tried to take a shower, but others had beaten me to it and all the water was gone. Keep in mind that the climate there is tropical. I was getting rancid and I am sure was beginning to smell. I decided I was going to get a shower regardless. I took my bar of green, Palmolive soap and got up very early to be the first into that shower. I turned on the water and soaped up from head to foot. Then the water went off. Not enough rain! There I stood in my birthday suit, lathered from head to toe and no water to rinse it off. I took my towel and did the best I could to dry myself. But it left a thin, sticky film all over me. At the building that morning, I managed to preach all right. But when it came my turn to speak that afternoon, it was plenty hot. The church building had a tin roof, no cooling system, and what air might flow in from the windows was partially blocked by crowds standing outside and looking through the windows to hear the preaching. I had already learned to take a small towel with me in the pulpit. By the time I would finish in the afternoon, there would not be a dry strand of clothes left on me and the towel would be soaked. Well, that afternoon, as I preached and began to sweat and then wipe it with the towel, it began to foam all over my face. Some of the Filipinos were greatly amused. After the session ended that afternoon, we had to walk about a mile back to Foranda's Place to get ready for the evening debate. On the way, one of the preachers said, "I like to watch brother Adam (most of them had trouble with the "s" on the end of my name) preach. He really gets excited and looks like a mad dog. That sermon really 'lathered' good." All I can say is that was the stickiest feeling I ever had.

A Jealous Preacher?

One of the most interesting assignments I have had was to prepare and deliver a speech at the Florida College lectures on "C.R. Nichol, Princely Preacher." I had met him when he came to Marietta, Georgia for a gospel meeting. He was then near eighty years old and made an impressive appearance. He stood ramrod straight, his glistening white hair was a becoming adornment and his delivery was arresting. He earlier had spoken to the Sower's Club at Florida College. When he walked up on the platform, he stumbled, his hair was in disarray, his shirt tail partly out, his coat was uneven on his shoulders, and his outer coat pocket was crammed full of combs and pens and pencils. We were all stunned, for we had been told how dignified a preacher he was. When he reached the speaker's stand, he said, "Now, young men, you have seen a demonstration of how *not* to mount the rostrum." Brother Nichol had three hundred debates with various teachers of error. The *Nichol's Pocket Bible Encyclopedia* has sold millions of copies and has been spread all over the world. I interviewed several brethren who had known C.R. Nichol well. One of these was Cleo Blue of Republic, Missouri. I spent a day with him as he reminisced about brother Nichol.

He related an incident in which Nichol was called for a meeting with a church that had a problem they hoped he could help them solve. They had no full time preacher. One of the men had made a short talk and decided he was ready to evangelize the world. He wanted to fill the pulpit and did such a poor job that people would go elsewhere when they heard that he was to speak. But he persisted. The brethren appealed to brother Nichol to talk to the man. Whether reluctantly or not, I do not know, but he did go to see him. He reasoned with him from 1 Corinthians 12:14-31 and pointed out that in the body of Christ, we do not all have the same abilities and function, that some can teach classes, some can lead singing, and some can preach, but that the Lord did not expect every man to preach. He tried to show him there were many things he could do in the Lord's service besides preaching. When the brother saw where Nichol was headed with his argument, he stopped him and said, "C. R. Nichol, I see what your trouble is. You're just jealous of me." Well, it takes all kinds.

"Bring Your Lunch"

During a meeting in coal mining country, I was asked to arbitrate a dispute between two men in the congregation. One accused the other of crowding his wife off a narrow road with his pickup truck. The driver of the truck in question said the other brother had threatened to "whip him." I got them together, finally, and asked if that was true. It seems that they did meet outside the entrance to the mine and words were exchanged. When one offered to "whip" the other, he replied, "I hope you brought your lunch, because it is gonna be an all day job." The situation had a happy ending. But, you know, some things do take longer than others.

Preaching in the Dark

At Marshall's Branch, about twenty-five miles south of Pikeville, in southeastern Kentucky, a thunder storm developed about the time services began. While we were singing, the lights flickered off and on two or three times. When I arose to speak I assured them that, if the lights went out, that I could preach in the dark. Well, I had hardly finished saying that before I had a chance to prove it! The lights not only went out there, but all over that area, and stayed out for several hours. I kept preaching but it was a little difficult. You see, I was preaching a two part sermon on "The Church Through the Ages" and had a large cloth chart for my "visual aid." What good is a visual aid which nobody can see? One of the brethren (I think he was a coon hunter) went out to his truck and came back with a large flashlight which had a big spotlight effect. He gave it to the preacher who sat on the front row and focused it on my chart and the sermon went on as planned. The only trouble with that is that you can't tell who goes to sleep. And come to think of it, there have been many through the years who thought my preaching was in the dark anyhow.

The Penitent Hound

I was to preach again in a meeting at McArthur Heights, near Jasper, Alabama where my long time friend, Thomas O'Neal, preached. He wrote and asked if I could come a few days earlier and preach a few nights in a brother's yard in the north end of Walker County. Brother Holley and his family were driving across the county to McArthur Heights and they were interested in trying to start a congregation in his end of the county. I agreed. Tom was to lead the singing and I was to stay with him during both meetings. Brother Holley was a farmer. His house was of rough lumber, unpainted and without any underpinning for the house. It stood high off the ground on brick pillars. Underneath the house he stored feed for livestock and it provided a haven for chickens and for dogs. Out on a sloping side yard, he had made some benches and arranged them like a small amphitheater. There was no  pulpit stand. He nailed a board across an oak tree to which I fastened a cloth chart each night. Brother Holley had a big hound dog with long floppy ears and sad eyes. While we were singing, the hound would come from under the house right down to the front row and lie there until I started preaching. He did not care much for my preaching and would get up and slowly amble back up under the house. Then, when we started singing the invitation song (we had forty to fifty people present each night), he would get up, shake himself, wander back down to the front, lie down almost at my feet, and look up at me with the saddest, most penitent looking face you ever saw. The first night, that happened, I did not dare to look at Tom and he did not look at me. I think both of us were afraid we might lose composure. Neither of us mentioned it on the way back to his house. But the second night, the same identical thing happened. On the way home that night, Tom could stand it no longer. He said, "Connie, you restored that old hound last night, but it didn't take, did it?" That became a routine every night and Tom told the folks at McArthur Heights that we had a restoration every night at brother Holley's yard.

Keeping A Sense of Humor

My good friend, Weldon Warnock, has macular degeneration and has lost all but some peripheral vision. But that has not dampened his spirit. He said that his vision troubles had actually helped his golf game since he could hit the ball out of sight every time. I have also had my share of vision problems over the years. In 2007, a surgical procedure to correct a problem about pressure from glaucoma in my right eye resulted in a hemorrhage which left me with only slight peripheral sight in that eye. Thankfully, I still have one good eye. But it reminds me of the fellow I heard about who only had one eye. He went to a show and argued that they ought to let him in for half price since he could only see half as much. But they ended up charging him double since they claimed it would take him twice as long to see it. The moral of all this? Nobody likes to be around a whiner. Bobby and I have learned to cherish the company of young people. They don't talk about their cholesterol, their medications, and their operations. Indeed, "a merry heart doeth good like a medicine."

Sometimes there is even humor to be found in the saddest of occasions. I heard about a Tennessee preacher who was asked to conduct a graveside service way out in the country. He got lost and was almost frantic at the thought of letting the family down. Finally, he spotted two men with a backhoe up on a hillside covering up some ground. He hurried up there. Nobody was there but these two men and their backhoe. He felt terrible about being late, but decided that, whether the family was present or not, he ought to read some Scripture and have a prayer. When he drove off, one of the backhoe operators said to the other, "You know, I've put down a lot of septic tanks in my time, but this beats anything I ever saw."

Chapter 14

The Printed Page

In addition to editing church bulletins where we have done local work, I have been much involved in writing for various periodicals. I have always considered such work an extension of my efforts to teach the word of God. My first published article was in 1951 in a paper called *Lifeline* which was edited for a short time by Pat Hardeman. In1973, not long before I began editing and publishing *Searching The Scriptures*, I had lunch one day with a fellow preacher in Louisville. He asked me what in the world possessed me to want to be involved in such an activity. My answer was simple. "I want to be able to teach the word of God 100 years after I am dead." I explained to him that most of us had in our libraries, the works of men which had been written well over 100 years in periodicals. I prize the bound volumes of periodicals brethren have published more highly than most of my other books. The material published not only provides good material for study and growth, but also supplies a history of the times in which the writers lived and the issues with which they had to grapple. There is a sentiment found among many that says, in effect, "Fooey on all these papers. They just stir up trouble." I realize that not all writing is worthwhile and that there have been papers published to ride hobbies or grind personal axes. But there is a legitimate place for journals to teach the truth, refute error, and provide forums for discussion of differences and forward news of interest to a wider audience.

The Gospel Guardian

In the fall of 1954, while in Indianapolis, Indiana at the Holt-Totty debate, Yater Tant, then editor of the *Gospel Guardian*, asked me to submit some articles to that paper. At the ripe old age of twenty-four, I did not think I had much to say that would be worth reading, but decided to do the best I could. My first article in that paper was entitled "Preaching Christ." To my surprise, brother Tant published it on the front page of the December 2, 1954 edition. That was the first of many articles which appeared in that paper until the early 1960's. Yater Tant was an able editor. He was a writer of both style and substance. Perhaps his most widely read columns were those he called "The Overflow." It was a mixture of short pieces which had a punch and oftentimes a humorous twist. Brother Tant was always kind to me. He printed every article I ever sent and was actively involved in helping raise support for our work in Norway. He also publicized the work there and kept readers informed as to the progress being made. That was one factor in encouraging some who followed us in Norway to come and devote several years to the work there.

During the heat of the battle over institutionalism and sponsoring churches, the *Gospel Guardian* was despised and belittled by those of a more liberal bent. Some of them referred to it as "The Gospel Garbage" and spoke of writers as "The *Guardian* Boys." B. C. Goodpasture, editor of the *Gospel Advocate*, proposed that a "yellow tag of quarantine" be affixed to those in sympathy with the "anti" views. He ran a confessional column in the *Advocate* in which a number of preachers sought to distance themselves from the hated "antis." Ads seeking preachers often said, "No anti need apply." It had an effect in drawing lines between brethren and causing some preachers to be fired and many had meetings cancelled. Some of those who wrote often in the *Gospel Guardian* were Roy E. Codgill, James W.

Adams, Luther Blackmon, Robert Farish, Robert Welch, Cecil B. Douthitt, Charles A. Holt, Hoyt Houchen, and several other worthies. Roy E. Cogdill perhaps paid as heavy a price for his convictions as anyone. He was invited to preach in meetings in the largest churches in the country and appeared often on college lecture programs. Many of those invitations disappeared. The paper ran a book store and printing business in Lufkin, Texas, largely to underwrite the cost of the magazine. Efforts were made to boycott that business. A few years ago, while in a meeting at Duncan, Oklahoma, C. R. Scroggins, took Bobby and me to the cemetery in Hobart, Oklahoma to visit the grave of Roy E. Cogdill. On his gravestone are found these appropriate words: "Buy the truth and sell it not" (Prov. 23:23).

I subscribed to the *Gospel Guardian*, as well as to the *Gospel Advocate* and the *Firm Foundation*. and read them all with interest, but it was the *Guardian* which helped me the most, as a young preacher, to review the arguments pro and con and which drove me to search the Scriptures and to resolve to stand on that ground whatever the cost. In later years, editor Tant launched what he called a "peace offensive" and tried to find some common ground on which we could all stand without compromising any point of truth. While his motives were admirable, those who had boarded the institutional bandwagon wanted no part of it. They were in the majority and willing to isolate and write off "antis." Brother Tant proposed a plan called "The box in the vestibule" so that brethren in a congregation, who wanted to send donations to one of the orphan homes, might do so without the treasury of the church being involved. But having such an institution in the budget had become a litmus test of brotherhood correctness and, with only a few notable exceptions, the plan was more derided than accepted. I wrote a piece in *Searching The Scriptures* entitled "The Mailbox on the Corner" and suggested that anyone who wanted to send a private donation to an orphan home or a college could utilize the mail service.

Brother Tant later edited *Vanguard* which, while carrying some good material, lacked the punch and distinctiveness of the *Guardian* in the 1950's and early 1960's. Though I wrote several articles critical of editor Tant's "peace offensive" and his contacts with the early Crossroads movement, we remained friends. I wrote to him several times in his old age and thanked him for the help he had extended to me when I was a young preacher. While I questioned his judgment in some of his efforts in his later years, I never doubted the sincerity of his motives. The last time I saw Yater Tant was in Murfreesboro, Tennessee where I was holding a meeting at Northfield Boulevard. He was in town to see an audiologist about his severe hearing loss. He thanked me for the sermon and said, "It had that old Jerusalem ring."

Truth Magazine

In the early 1960's I wrote some articles which were published in *Searching The Scriptures* (of which I have many things to say, later). I had great respect for H. E. Phillips who edited that paper with the help of James P. Miller who had been a friend for sometime. Two series were put together in booklet form and both of them have gone through numerous printings and are still being used. One was *Premillennialism, True or False?* The other was *Miraculous Di-*

vine Healing, Faith or Fake? Truth Magazine asked if they could publish these as book-lets and brother Phillips and I both agreed. They are still marketed by Guardian of Truth Foundation.

When we moved to Akron, Ohio in 1965, I was asked to serve as an Associate Editor of *Truth Magazine* along with James P. Need-ham, William Wallace, and Earl Robertson. As indicated earlier, the Akron years were busy and fruitful in many ways. Working with Cecil Willis at Brown Street was pleas-ant and gave us opportunity to discuss many things which had to do with the magazine and topics which needed to be addressed. I was called on to deal with a number of difficult issues. The work with *Truth Magazine* continued for eight years, un-til I left the staff to edit *Searching The Scriptures*. It was during the eight years I served in that capacity that twenty brethren met in Memphis, Tennessee for the first of two meetings to discuss the need for a graded series of literature written by those not connected with institutionalism. Much of what was being used was weak doctrinally and some of it taught error. William E. Wallace helped to arrange that meeting. In that, and later meetings with brethren who were involved in operating bookstores and in publication work, it was agreed that Roy E. Cogdill should serve as editor-in-chief of this major project. He agreed provided they would agree to have Ferrell Jenkins and Cecil Willis to serve as co-editors of this major undertaking. All agreed with that plan. Cecil helped to raise funds while Ferrell attended to the work of editing and coordinating the writing. It took longer than originally planned and cost over $100,000. The series, named *Truth in Life*, was often used in connection with the revised series *Walking with God*. For many years these two series were widely used. Both of them have now been revised and continue to be useful. Some brethren have also prepared and marketed other useful class material.

I continued my association with *Truth Magazine* for eight years until I left the staff to edit *Searching The Scriptures* in June, 1973. In an editorial in *Truth* dated May 31, 1973, editor Willis wrote these kind words:

> Frequently some unpleasant writing task has needed to be done. I have not shunned to attend to my share of such distasteful chores. But when more of such

unappreciated tasks appeared than I could attend to, Connie Adams was one of the first of those to whom I turned with an unpleasant writing assignment. The rebuking of errorists and the exposure of error frequently is a thankless job. Not once did Connie ever flinch from such an assignment. . . . A man accepts such assignments at the expense of personal popularity with some, but Connie never hesitated to say what needed to be said. Such a man at your side is much appreciated and will be much missed.

In my severance article, published in the same issue, I wrote the following:

I am anxious for all readers of both papers to know that the ending of my work with this paper signals no breach in friendship with Cecil Willis or any other writers on the staff of *Truth Magazine*. I am as much committed to the aims of this paper as ever. My convictions touching subjects on which I have written in this medium are unchanged. I am not assuming editorship of *Searching The Scriptures* with any sort of bad taste in my mouth or with an intention of grinding any personal axes.

Searching The Scriptures

In1958, H. E. Phillips and James P. Miller, in an attempt to prevent brethren in Florida from dividing, began the *Florida Newsletter*. This soon expanded to the *Southeastern Newsletter*. It carried news of interest to churches throughout the region and began to also print editorials which did not please some of the readers. In the fall of 1959 interested brethren met in Orlando and plans were laid to begin *Searching The Scriptures* as a twelve-page monthly periodical. H. E. Phillips would be the editor and James P. Miller was, at first, listed as co-editor. Brother Miller traveled widely in gospel meetings and worked diligently to build a subscription list. He referred to their relationship as "Mr. Inside" and "Mr. Outside." Throughout the southeast, as well as other parts of the country, a bias had developed toward the *Gospel Guardian* so that many brethren, who did not know what the "issues" were all about, would not even read it. Many preachers cautioned them against reading it. But both James P. Miller and H. E. Phillips had considerable influence with many brethren whom they thought could be shown the truth, if they would just get past their prejudice and read. From the first issue in January, 1960, the paper had a punch and took on a unique personality. It soon expanded to sixteen pages. Editorials by brother Phillips were hard hitting but written in a brotherly spirit. Brother Miller wrote a popular column entitled "I Marvel" in which he often flagged some of the strange things happening among brethren who were drifting from the truth. The paper chose some writers whose work appeared under column headings which gave them latitude to deal with a wide range of things. Soon, readers developed a

special affinity for certain column writers and looked eagerly for their material.
Marshall E. Patton took on the task of
writing "Answers for Our Hope," a question and answer column. The first twenty
years of that column were later published
in a book under that name. It remains a
useful tool in researching any number
of Bible subjects. Edgar Srygley wrote a
word study column. Ward Hogland, Eu-
gene Britnell, Thomas G. O'Neal, and
others wrote under assigned headings.
The bulk of the material in each issue was
from those who were asked to write under

these headings, but other material was welcomed, as well. From the beginning,
the paper had balance and efforts were made to be fair when dealing with mat-
ters of controversy.

The paper reached a circulation at one time of over 11,000, the largest of
any of the non-institutional papers. When I became editor in June, 1973, the
circulation was still at 7,200. The subscription rate was modest and there were
a number who paid for subscriptions for friends and family members. But the
publication took its toll. While Phillips Publications sold books, tapes, and
supplies, it did not always offset the expense. Brother Phillips ended up bor-
rowing against his life insurance to pay printing bills.

In the May, 1973 issue H. E. Phillips wrote of the history of the paper and
then of my involvement with it. Let him tell it in his own words.

> Somewhere around 1963-1965, during the Lecture Week at Florida College late
> one night, I drove Connie Adams to the place where he was staying after the
> last lecture that night. We spent almost an hour talking about *Searching The
> Scriptures* and its future, and about the need for some continuing force to fight
> the invading evils of institutionalism and liberalism. It was on this night and
> under these circumstances that Connie W. Adams asked me to give him first
> opportunity to buy *Searching The Scriptures* if I ever sold it. At the time I had
> not thought of ever selling it. However, I gave him my word that I would contact
> him first under such circumstances, and through the years our verbal agreement
> has been honored by both of us. After two heart attacks, one on January 1, 1967,
> and the second on August 3, 1971, my doctor, my wife, my children, my mother,
> my brothers, my brethren, the elders at Forest Hills, and almost all who knew me

urged that I surrender this work for my health's sake. After reluctantly accepting the fact that they were right, I contacted my beloved brother, Connie Adams, in January of this year (1973, CWA) and told him the situation. After some careful, prayerful thought by him and his wife, he agreed to take this tremendous responsibility. . . . I know of no man in whose hands I would rather see this work go, which symbolizes to me the labor of nearly fourteen years of my life, than into the hands of Connie W. Adams.

I quote what he and Cecil Willis wrote, not because they praised me, but to historically document the circumstances under which I left the staff of *Truth Magazine* and then took on the work of editing *Searching The Scriptures*. There is a tendency for some to suspect that there is some skeleton in the closet when a brother leaves his work with one publishing business and then takes up a similar effort elsewhere. When H. E. Phillips called me, the timing could not have been worse for me. We had just made plans to go with the new congregation at Hebron Lane, had borrowed money to build a house, and had our plate full. My wife, Bobbie, had been teaching school and agreed to leave that work and take on the business and office work for the paper. That was great help for she taught business education courses to high school juniors and seniors.

In the late spring of 1973, Tom O'Neal and I drove to Atlanta and met with H. E. Phillips and one of the elders from Forest Hills in Tampa. We spent the night and the better part of two days discussing the challenges, opportunities, and blessings of such work, not to mention the awesome responsibility involved. I asked for, and received, much good advice. We prayed together several times. It was a sobering meeting. Brother Phillips knew what he had to do, but I honestly believe it would have been easier for him to bury a beloved family member than to part with that work. Ed Byers, of Louisville, went to Tampa with me to bring the physical property of the business to its new home. After we had loaded the U-Haul trailer, Elwood (friends called him that) asked to lead a prayer for our safety and for the future success of the paper. As we drove away, we left Elwood and Polly Phillips standing in the door of their home weeping. Neither Ed nor I could say a word for several miles.

Several have asked me what I had to pay to purchase the paper. In many ways the paper had great worth. How many lives had been touched for good in those first thirteen and one-half years, only eternity will reveal. But monetarily it had little value. Brother Phillips had borrowed $10,000 against his life insurance. I agreed to pay that amount over a three year period. With the dedicated help of my wife, we were able to pay what we had agreed and had the business in the black in three years. I decided I was not going to operate it at a loss. I did not have the funds to start a book store. An agreement was reached with Religious Supply Center in Louisville for them to purchase two pages of advertising space in each issue of the paper. This business was operated by David Key and was a stock holding business formed by several Christians in Louisville. Our working relationship was pleasant in every way. They needed to reach a wider market and we needed their business. We also sold ad space for churches so travelers could locate them.

We expanded the paper to twenty pages and then finally to twenty-four. Increased printing and mailing costs forced us to raise the subscription price several times. We had it printed at Berne, Indiana, mainly because I could not find a printer who would match their price, and besides, I already was acquainted with them since they had printed *Truth Magazine* and Guardian of Truth Foundation books and literature for several years. For about five years, I drove to Berne each month to haul the paper to Brooks for addressing and mailing. That was a five hour trip, one way. Berne is near Ft. Wayne, Indiana. They would load it at the plant, filling the trunk and back seat of a full sized car. Then we bought a large station wagon. In the process we had to replace the universal joint, I also developed back problems from unloading those boxes, then reloading thirty-eight to forty mail sacks, and then unloading them at the Post Office, handling all that weight three times each month. The doctor said I tore up my own universal joint which required surgery twice and still gives me problems at times. I finally decided to have them address it at the plant and mail it from Berne.

Publishing was considerably different from 1973-1992 than it is now. I had two deadlines a month. At the first of each month I sent typed manuscripts to the printer. Two weeks later they would return to me printed galley sheets the width of a column in the paper. I would then do a paste-up. I would take a previous issue of the paper, change the dates and page numbers, and then cut and paste articles so I could see where they would appear. We used the gaps at the ends of articles for ad space for the book store. That would be returned to the printer and they would do the finished product. I kept a backlog of manuscripts, usually enough to publish the paper for the next year or more. Most of the articles which appeared were from the column writers, but we tried to include several others as we had space. Some articles did not deserve to be printed. Sometimes an article would be kept back because we had recently printed one on the same subject. I asked writers to prepare their material with the ordinary Christian in mind. We did not pretend to be a journal pitched on such an intellectual level that common people would not be able to understand it. Writers were expected to respect our space limitations. If they were reviewing what someone else had said or written, I asked them to be sure they clearly understood what the other person had said or written, to represent it fairly, and not to make personal attacks. There were several times when I returned articles to the senders who did not respect those requirements.

Deciding what controversies to air and how long they should be extended was always difficult. We had several exchanges between brethren who took divergent views on issues of importance. I decided that, in such cases, the exchange would be limited to three articles apiece and then we would put the matter to rest and go on to something else. It was our aim to keep the paper well balanced. We did not always succeed, but that was the goal. We had a number of special issues which we usually ran in July. Some of these required extra printings. The special we did on "The Family Under Fire" had an enlarged printing to begin with but had to be reprinted three times to satisfy the demand. In hindsight, there are some things I would have done differently, but always did what I honestly thought was the best thing at the time.

After Bobbie died, Donnie and Joan Rader came to my rescue with the office work. Donnie edited several issues for me when I had surgery and during one summer to give me a needed break. Without their help, the paper would have gone out of business much sooner. After Bobby 2 and I married, she worked in the office along with Joan Rader when she was not traveling with me to meetings. After their daughter was born, Joan needed to be at home and we employed Jane Ashbrook, the daughter of A. C. Grider and wife of Lee Ashbrook, then an elder at Manslick Road. After her father died, she took on the care of her mother and asked to be relieved of her work. We then engaged the services of Karen Arbuckle, whose husband was a deacon at Manslick Road. All of these did excellent work. The last year we were in business, we lost a little and ended up in the red. Our mailing list was then near 5,000. Over time, older readers died, others, who had been paying for lists of readers, grew older and were on limited incomes and had to cut back on expenses. The computer age has taken a heavy toll on the print media in general, including religious journals. A younger generation does not read as much as the preceding ones did.

In February, 1992, during the Florida College lectures, at which I was one of the speakers, James D. Yates approached me to talk about merging my efforts

Connie with H. E. Phillips. A surprise appreciation dinner at Luby's Cafeteria, Tampa, Florida, February, 1993. We were presented plaques for our work as editors of *Searching The Scriptures*. This was arranged by Tom O'Neal and Donnie Rader.

with *Truth Magazine*. Brother Yates was on the board of the Guardian of Truth Foundation. At first, I told him I was not interested. But then, after thinking about it and discussing it with Bobby 2 and then with H. E. Phillips, I decided to meet with them to discuss it. We all agreed that both papers were on the same page as far as issues concerning brethren were involved. I had worked with *Truth Magazine* for eight years as noted earlier. I was well acquainted with those who made up the Foundation board. I had some differences with a couple of writers on some aspects of the marriage, divorce and remarriage issue. I believed, and still do, that only the one *who put away* the other for fornication, had a right to remarry, and that the one put away had no such right. I also believed, and still do, that fornication is the *only* reason for which one may divorce. All of us believed and preached that fornication is the only reason for divorce and remarriage. I stated my concerns and we had three meetings in all to air out the issue. I told them that if what I considered to be the "mental divorce" position (putting one away in purpose of heart after a legal divorce has occurred) was taught in the paper, then I would feel obligated to oppose it. To a man, they all said they would not have it any other way and that I would not be limited in what I could say on that or any other matter. It was that understanding which gave rise to the exchange which I had later with my long-time friend, Weldon Warnock.

After much thought and prayer, I decided not to continue the publication of *Searching The Scriptures* after December, 1992. That completed thirty-three years of service for the paper. It was my thought that it would be better to give it a respectable burial myself than to run the risk of having it one day fall into hands who would take it where neither H. E. Phillips nor I would have wanted it to go. His own counsel on the matter was critical in making that decision. Thanks to the efforts of Donnie V. Rader, all issues of *Searching The Scriptures* are now on a website which Donnie owns: www.searchingthescriptures.com as well as truthmagazine.com. I am glad that the labors of thirty-three years have been preserved in this way and that generations to come will have access to this material.

At this late date, I still meet people during meetings who subscribed to that paper and who remember specific articles. Hundreds of copies of it have circulated in the Philippines (and other countries) and I have met men who told me the paper played a key role in their conversion. Others will have to judge the effects of this work. It was hard for me to prepare the final issue of the paper. Here were my closing words in the December, 1992 issue.

> If we have helped one soul to learn the truth and obey the gospel, if we have strengthened one Christian, if we have stabilized one soul on the brink of apostasy, if we have lifted one despondent spirit, if we have illuminated one Bible student on some difficult passage, if we have promoted greater zeal and interest in the work of the gospel around the world, then these 33 years have not been in vain. So then, with a heart filled with emotions, and with gentle hands, we commit *Searching The Scriptures* to the archives of history. "And now brethren, I commend you to God, and to the word of his grace, which is able to build you up, and to give you an inheritance among all them which are sanctified" (Acts 20:32). "The grace of our Lord Jesus Christ be with you all. Amen" (Rev. 22:21).

Truth Magazine, Again

When the decision was made to close down the publication of *Searching*

The Scriptures, I agreed to merge the mailing list with that of *Truth Magazine* and *Truth* was to fulfill all subscriptions. Several of the writers for *Searching The Scriptures* agreed to submit articles to *Truth*. I was asked to serve again as Associate Editor and also to serve on the board of the Truth Foundation. The board meets twice a year and has much business to handle relative to the publishing concerns. One thing which was of special interest to me was the *Truth Commentaries* being planned and published. There had not been a commentary series on the New Testament since the *Gospel Advocate Commentaries* published in the late 1930's and early 1940's. The project has developed over about twenty-five years and is nearing completion on the part involving the New Testament. At this writing there are five New Testament books to be completed and work is finished on the majority of that with target dates in sight. Four commentaries have been written on the Old Testament. These commentaries are in matching bindings, attractive in appearance, and meaty in substance. They are useful study tools which should benefit Bible students for many years to come. In addition to that project, we have revised and repackaged the *Truth in Life* and *Walking with God* series of graded literature. We have published some of the best material available for adult Bible classes. The *Bible Text Book* series now covers every book in the Bible except Psalms and work is being done on that, at this writing. A major new hymnal will soon be published, in conjunction with *Sumphonia*. We have published many books by writers of the current generation and have brought back into print many works which were out of print but which need to be kept available. The Foundation has two book stores, Truth Bookstore in Bowling Green, Kentucky and CEI in Athens, Alabama, from which we market our own publications as well as that of other publishers.

The board consists of nine men with five currently acting as advisers. Five board members are elders of the churches where they worship. Some of us are gospel preachers. Three are very able businessmen (and two of them are also elders where they live and worship). The present board is congenial and business is conducted in a dignified and honorable fashion. Mike Willis has served as editor of the paper for over thirty years. My work with him has been pleasant. He often calls me for advice and I offer what I hope will help. Final decisions as to what material to print in the magazine are his. We have not agreed on everything which has

Mike Willis

come before us, but we have been able, as brethren, to work through differences of view in an open and honorable way. Mike is a diligent student and a man of deep conviction and upright character. What many people do not realize is that the magazine is among the smallest parts of what the foundation does.

For many years the magazine and the foundation have been under fire from several quarters. There have been some who have devoted much of their time and effort to destroying the influence of those who have been connected with the paper and the foundation. We have been accused, both directly and subtly, of trying to dominate the brotherhood. Special editions of other periodicals have been published to discredit our work. For several years, speakers on the lectures at Florida College have gone out of their way to make sarcastic or snide remarks clearly aimed at our work. We are certainly not above criticism and I, for one, recognize that over time the best judgment may not have been exercised in dealing with various issues. But the notion that we are a bunch of thugs who meet in secret conclaves to plot and scheme about how to manage or manipulate the brotherhood is totally without foundation. What is the genesis of these false impressions?

During the heat of the controversy over the grace-unity movement spawned by W. Carl Ketcherside and aided and abetted among non-institutional brethren by Edward Fudge and the young men he influenced, a number of feathers were ruffled. Edward Fudge was the son of the beloved Bennie Lee Fudge of Athens, Alabama. Bennie Lee Fudge, for many years operated the C.E.I. bookstore in Athens. He had a daily radio program and preached for a number of churches in that county. When he took his stand against the *Herald of Truth*, after hearing the Holt-Nichols debate, the powers at Fifth and Highland in Abilene, Texas, which sponsored the Herald of Truth, turned on him with full force. They boycotted his bookstore in Abilene and tried to disrupt his business in Athens. Bennie Lee Fudge had much to do with so many congregations in north Alabama standing against institutionalism and centralization in the work of the church. The work we did in Norway was greatly helped by Bennie Lee Fudge when he underwrote the translation and printing costs for the entire C.E.I. literature series to be used there. Edward Fudge was his oldest son. He was bright and scholarly by inclination.

As a young man, and still a student at Florida College, he began writing articles which appeared in a number of periodicals. In time, his work could be seen in papers published by liberal brethren and also those in the Christian Church. On the campus of Florida College he circulated *Mission Messenger* among some of the students. This was published by W. Carl Ketcherside. Also, he spread around *Restoration Review* a publication of Leroy Garrett, a fellow traveler with W. Carl Ketcherside. These men at one time were radicals who opposed a located preacher, a stipulated salary for preachers, and also the right of a school like Florida College to even exist. They advocated what was called "mutual edification" and evangelistic oversight. Garrett had a debate with Bill Humble (which is in print) in which he argued against the right of the college to teach the Bible. He argued that this was the exclusive work of the local church and also railed against the college lecture program, calling it "a gospel meeting." But, these two radicals then went to the other extreme and began to advocate fellowship between all factions of what was called the Restoration movement, including premillennialists, institutionalists, and the Christian Church. They said that we are all children of God in error, but just on different things. They advocated unity on the ground that the grace of God, as a giant spiritual umbrella would reach out to cover all these nuances. They applied Romans 14 to all of these doctrinal errors. They made a distinction in the "core gospel" and the doctrine of Christ. They argued that doctrinal differences should not limit fellowship.

These views had far reaching ripples. While I was preaching at Manslick Road in the early 1970's, we had several young people who were attending Florida College and some of them began attending services at a congregation in Tampa where there were no elders and where some of the students took a leading part, including some infected with this virus. I had written against some of this in *Truth Magazine* in the late 1960's and early 1970's. I thought the matter serious enough that I called together the parents of the young people then attending school there, and warned them of the dangers involved. So far as I know, none of those young people was carried away with the error. (This movement among students was not sanctioned by the faculty or administration of the college.) James W. Adams wrote an extended series of articles in *Truth Magazine* dealing with this error and identifying by name some of those caught up in it. As a historical footnote, most of the ones he identified, plus some others, ended up leaving the truth. Some went into liberalism and some to the Christian Church or into other denominations.

But the very idea of a paper printing articles critical of Edward Fudge was more than some could stand. The friends and parents of some other involved young people might not have understood, or might not have agreed if they did understand, the doctrinal issues involved, but blood and friendship are pretty thick. Besides that, there had been a growing aversion to controversy.

The Plot Thickens

The *Gospel Guardian* had fallen on hard times. William E. Wallace took on the task of editing that paper, and formed an alliance with C.E.I. bookstore. Edward Fudge became Associate Editor of the *Gospel Guardian*. It was an uneasy bond. Brother Wallace found himself in the position of trying to defend Edward Fudge. He made a trip which he said was "to feel the pulse of the brotherhood" and, at every stop, had to answer questions about Edward Fudge. In the meantime in the November 22, 1973 issue of the *Gospel Guardian*, he wrote an editorial entitled "The Political Mr. Willis" in which he charged that Cecil Willis aspired to be "the titular head of his own church of Christ." He further claimed that this controversy had been kept alive in an effort to corner the literature business of all the brethren. In the January, 1974 issue of *Searching The Scriptures* I wrote the following:

> The conflict reached a new low plane and the principal issue was obscured when editor Wallace wrote an article entitled "The Political Mr. Willis" in which he charged that Cecil Willis aspires to be "the titular head of his own church of Christ." For shame! It is one thing to ask pointed questions as to where people stand and another to impute sinister motives. Editor Wallace has had much to say about fairness, kindness and brotherly love and how the absence of these "turn off" younger preachers. Do such allegations as he has made reflect the virtues he has so ardently recommended in others? Even if he believes in his heart that they are true, does it contribute to fellowship, unity and love to say these things out loud? Either his recommendation is wrong or else his practice is.

> On December 3, 1973 William Wallace spoke to a fair sized audience in Louisville, Kentucky on "The Past, Present and Future of the *Gospel Guardian*." . . .I urged brother Wallace during the question period to offer his apology for the severe impugning of motives which he had done. He refused to do so. I told him after the session that I was going to appeal to him in this paper to do so. He owes it to brother Willis and to a brotherhood embarrassed to see such a spirit injected into what should be a controversy over Bible teaching, and especially from one who has deplored "ugly journalism." Personal reflections would best be left out by all parties concerned. A book business is not the issue. The size or circulation of a paper is not the issue. The aspirations, or lack of them, of editors is not the issue. There are real, spiritual issues at stake which may only be settled by an appeal to what the Bible says. While there is room for discussion as to the best judgment with which to pursue these problems, it is one thing to deal with doctrine and its tendencies and another to malign the motives of those who ask questions about where one stands and about what one has written.

I do not recall reading any other rebuke of such ugly charges beyond what

I wrote and what appeared in *Truth Magazine*. But this was the genesis of the impression that has been formed and encouraged by those who have bought into the idea that *Truth Magazine* is a bully and out to control the brotherhood and that those of us who write for it are a bunch of conniving thugs.

Another episode which engendered ill will toward the foundation was the decision to stop publishing *Pitching For The Master* which was edited by Lindy McDaniel. Lindy was a renowned baseball pitcher, a member of the church and highly esteemed. While he has distanced himself from earlier views which fostered doubts about his soundness, it is a fact that he became involved with Hubert A. Moss who followed the views of Edward Fudge and Carl Ketcherside all the way to the Christian Church. The Guardian of Truth Foundation was publishing Lindy's paper and when it became evident that views were being expressed which favored some aspects of the grace-unity movement, it was decided that they could no longer publish a paper which stood in opposition to what had been dealt with so plainly in *Truth Magazine*. Well, the fat was in the fire with a good many brethren who did not know what issues were involved and did not bother to find out. He was a folk hero to many young people. How dare the foundation stop publishing his paper and even leave doubts about his soundness! Again, I say that Lindy is not to be held accountable for what took place long ago and which he has rejected. He continues to preach, has done much good and has published some helpful study materials. I am sorry he got caught up in the controversy and so is he. But to put into perspective the origins of the lingering ill will which some, to this day, hold regarding the paper and the foundation, this could not be left out.

Falth Magazine

In January, 1974, a piece of literature was mailed out over the country and circulated on campus at Florida College during the lecture program. It was in the exact format of *Truth Magazine* and was published anonymously. Intended as a satire, it went far beyond that. The names of the editor and staff writers were scrambled as well as such men as W. Carl Ketcherside and Edward Fudge. It was an unmerciful assault on Cecil Willis and especially on James W. Adams who had written a series recently dealing with the grace-unity movement. In time, the publishers were discovered and were all young men who had been influenced by Ed-

ward Fudge, though he did not personally have anything to do with this sample of yellow journalism. It is interesting that all of those involved in this left the truth. Some went into outright liberalism and some to the Christian Church and other denominations. It is hard to describe the degree of malice and outright hatred this product manifested. One brother at the lectures that year was heard to say that he "had mixed feelings about *Falth Magazine*." Any brother with respect for truth and right should have been appalled at this slickly produced smear of good brethren. Satire is one thing, but this intruded into the realm of outright lies and serious impugning of motives.

But it did reflect the animosity which had built toward *Truth Magazine* for its exposure of the denominational error involved in the grace-unity movement and the danger this posed to the cause of our Lord. That spirit of resentment and disdain yet lingers and is expressed in somewhat more muted form in recent publications and gossip sessions in some preacher gatherings.

Recent Opposition

In the last few years, there have been a few men who have waged a relentless battle against the paper and foundation because of a lecture program which we have conducted in Bowling Green, Kentucky for the last five years. It is ordered very much like the lecture program at Florida College which has been provided annually since 1946. With few exceptions, little opposition has been raised against that program. The attendance at Bowling Green is small in comparison to the one in Tampa. Both Florida College and Guardian of Truth Foundation are private enterprises which offer teaching and instruction for sale. They provide it in the classroom and we do it in publishing work. The main contention of those who are critical of the lecture program seems to be that the local church is the only collective which can provide for Bible teaching or hymn singing. Why critics want to apply what they contend is a Bible principle to the Truth Magazine Lectures and not to other collective activities remains a mystery, unless they have bought into the unfounded impressions we have been discussing. For years there has been a singing school conducted by R. J. Stevens at Wilburton, Oklahoma. Several work together in this activity. There is a lecture series similar to the one we have in the northern Illinois area. Papers function to teach the Bible and receive contributed articles which become a part of what is sold in a subscription price. Funeral businesses provide facilities in which Christians gather and sing, pray, and preach. The church has no business contributing funds to private organizations. But when some devote web sites to opposing *only* the lectures in Bowling Green, or papers carry numerous articles to that end while saying absolutely nothing about other activities of the same nature, it raises questions as to why this activity has been singled out.

Indeed, a hundred years after I am dead, unless the Lord comes first, there will be some who will read not only some of my writing, but the many publications of the foundation will still be around as useful tools for serious Bible students. Looking back over sixty years of work in the kingdom, I know of nothing I have done which has the potential of doing more good in both the short and the long term, than being a part of the writing which I have been allowed to do and helping to plan and execute the publication of the careful study of a host of good people. If some choose to criticize or even to challenge my motives and those of brethren among whom time and circumstance have brought me into involvement, that will have to be between them and the Lord. I thank my God for opening doors to spread His word on the printed page.

Chapter 15

The Winds of Change

The world of today has changed dramatically from the one into which I was born in 1930. The world map has been redrawn over these years. Nations have changed their names and territorial boundaries have been either expanded or contracted. During this time our country has emerged from a great depression which began in 1929 and lasted until the beginning of World War II. We struggled through that war which lasted from December, 1941-August, 1945. It was a time of rationing of many things. My father had a coupon book with which he could purchase so much gasoline a week. Tires were at a premium. Sugar was scarce. We sweetened iced tea with Karo syrup. Our nation was at war and there was a general spirit of patriotism which inspired citizens to sacrifice on behalf of our men who were engaged in combat in both the Pacific and in Europe. We had blackouts and safety drills just in case the enemy should attack cities in our homeland. Even Hollywood was patriotic. The movies of the time reflected it. A number of actors joined the armed services. Truth be told, it was really World War II which ended the great depression.

The generation which survived that war picked up the pieces, went to work, and built this country into the most prosperous nation on earth. The price of the freedom and our way of life is to be seen in the military cemeteries which are found in Luzon in the Philippines, in France, and in Italy. I have stood in awe in Luzon and at Anzio, Italy and viewed the endless rows of crosses or stars of David, marking the resting places of those who gave all they had to give so we can be free. In 1949 the Korean War broke out. It ended in a virtual truce and we still have men deployed in Korea. Then came the Vietnam War which changed the face of America in a number of ways. That war spawned the hippy movement of the 1960's from which we have never recovered. University and college campuses became battle grounds. Protest music chronicled the discontent of a younger generation. Everything which was traditional or smacked of time-honored mores was turned upside down. Music and dress reflected a spirit of contempt for whatever the older set favored or revered. We have since had conflict in Bosnia, Afghanistan, and Iraq. But the spirit of patriotism which marked World War II has long since disappeared. One writer summarized it well. He said, "The marines and the army are at war. Americans are at the mall."

Changes in Transportation

Before the depression began, my father had a T-model Ford and then later a Dodge "touring car." But from the early 1930's until 1940, we did not have a car. We lived about two miles from Hopewell, Virginia in the woods. When my father could find work, he had to walk or hitch hike to get there and back. Once, he worked for several weeks dredging a canal off of the James River. He would leave home before daylight and return after dark. He had to walk several miles each way and was paid $1 a day. I remember walking to town with him to buy what groceries he could afford. He would put them in a burlap bag and bring them home over his shoulder. He bought bare necessities. When he could, he would bring home a little hard candy, but that was a treat.

There were no interstate highways until the 1950's. That system was begun during the Eisenhower administration. U.S. highways took you right through the heart of cities and towns. There were no McDonalds, Burger Kings, or Wendy's. While there were a few restaurants in towns and cities, many people, including us, packed a lunch and stopped beside the road to eat (hopefully under a shade tree in the summer). We learned to read maps and tried to find the shortest routes to wherever we had to go. If we had to travel very far, we often drove at night. There was not as much traffic and the car seemed to run better at night. If there were two drivers in the car, one would drive while the other tried to sleep. Bobbie 1 and I made a number of trips like that from Tampa to Fulton, Kentucky, or to Hopewell, Virginia. Both of these were 900 mile trips. Since interstates have been built, the distance has shortened by about forty miles in both cases. It took us twenty-one to twenty-three hours to make those trips. The next time you have an all day trip to make on an interstate highway, instead of being bored, count your blessings and be thankful for that endless ribbon of concrete without stop signs or traffic lights.

I never traveled by train in this country except that one trip when Martin Lemon and I first went to Florida Christian College. I did make some trips by bus. The first time I ever flew to a meeting was in 1956. I flew from Atlanta to Rocky Mount, North Carolina where my folks met me and drove me to Pike Road. This was my first meeting there since I had preached that first sermon there in 1945. I flew on Capital Airlines, a two engine prop. People used to dress up when they traveled by plane and some did when they went by bus. These days, a great many travelers dress down, way down. I have seen people in the most bizarre states of dress (and undress) at airports and on planes. In fact, if you have on a suit and tie, or even a sport jacket, you almost appear overdressed for the occasion. The Dixie Boys in our comedy act wore strange looking outfits on stage for comedic effect. Now, they would not appear out of the ordinary at the airport or the mall.

Bobby 2 and I still prefer to drive to our meetings whenever possible. The older you become, the more things you have to take along. We take our own pillows, and a bag of medical supplies in case of emergencies. We both have a large suitcase, each one has a suit bag (for hang-up clothes), each a brief case, Bobby has a cosmetic case (which I have labeled her "tackle box" since it contains her "lures"), a "goody bag" which sometimes has become a survival kit, and I always have papers to give away and some books to work with during the meeting. When we go to trade cars, the first thing I do is measure the trunk. If we can't get our things in it, we don't need it. Flying requires us to pack differently but it gets us there sooner. It is a hassle since September 11, 2001. Since I have not done local work since 1975, we don't have the time contraints which would demand that we always get home on Saturday. The time it takes to drive to our destination and to return home is precious time for us. Traffic is much heavier than it used to be and we have had to make some adjustments. We don't travel at night any more than is necessary. We enjoy driving in the west, traffic is much lighter and it is a great joy to us to pass through the miles of God's creation without contending with heavy traffic.

Societal Changes

There was a time when people did not lock their doors. There was no need for that. Everybody felt free to correct the neighbor's (or the brethren's) children when they were disrespectful without fear of a lawsuit. Rebellious children at school were paddled. It was expected. You were not allowed to curse your teacher, or even talk back. If you got paddled at school, you got another one from your parents when you got home. Children were not allowed to be disruptive in public, whether in a store, in a restaurant, at the doctor's office, at school, and certainly not at church. "Time out" or "I'm counting to ten" were not heard of. Common sense was far more common than it appears to be now. Most mothers were at home. One of the greatest societal changes over these decades may be summarized in the simple statement. "Mother isn't home." Our nation, and even the church, has paid a high price for this change.

Hospitality has undergone a drastic change during my lifetime. Many times I have sung an old country song "Company's Comin' Up the Road." Where we lived, if you saw car lights through the corn field, they were coming to our house. There was nowhere else to go up that road. My mother would say, "Somebody is coming, you kids pick up." That meant put things away and straighten up the house. That was a special time for me as a child. It meant we would have entertainment that night. There was no television. We would welcome whoever it was. The adults would sit around and talk and tell funny stories, or about strange things that happened, and the children would sit in the floor with big ears and listen. My Daddy would say to Mama, "Hon, could you make us a little fudge?" Yes sir, it was grand when company came. Did they call first? No, they did not have a phone and neither did we. Sometimes we would load up and go to one of the aunts or uncles. They were just as glad to see us. Sometimes we had company to stay two or three days. The old song about "Sleepin' at the Foot of the Bed" was more truth than fiction. I have slept in a bed with cousins when we slept crossways with three of us on the bed. You did not want to be at the foot.

During World War II, the congregation at Hopewell showed much hospitality to service men stationed at Fort Lee. We had some young men to come to services who were members of the church and they would often bring some of their friends along. Most of them were barely out of high school. Some were homesick, lovesick, or away from home for the first time in their lives. Some were fearful as to what awaited them when they shipped out. My folks, and others, resolved that every service man would be invited to go home with someone for dinner. Several times, Daddy took us home and would go back to town and bring home a carload of soldiers. It was good for them and for us. It was also educational to hear them tell about the place from which they came.

What changed all that? Television! If you did not have one, and happened to visit with a family which had acquired one, you had to respect the changed rules of the house. You only talked during commercials. It was a cardinal sin to talk during the show. Then gradually people became more mobile. As automobiles became more plentiful, fewer people might be found at home. As people had a little more money, they were able to go to the movie or to sporting events at the local high school. Modern conveniences seemed to make life busier and busier, but it slowed down hospitality.

Everything about "the good ole days" was not all it has been represented to be. We have idealized, and romanticized, if not glamorized the past. Everybody was not good. We had moonshiners, gangsters and crooked politicians. We had our Al Capones and John Dillingers. The dust bowl drove many Okies to California in search of a better life. While many of us are nostalgic about things we remember from years ago, there are some things I do not want to live with again. I'd much rather keep my indoor plumbing than revert to the outhouse. I have drawn as many buckets of water as I want to, from a thirty foot well with a rope on a pulley. We did not have central heat or air. In the summertime, it was so hot at night you would completely sweat out your night clothes. In the winter, it did not take long to get ready for bed and when you jumped in, you had to be careful to land where you wanted to sleep because you had so much heavy cover (usually home made quilts) that you had a hard job just turning over. I think I will just keep my electric blanket, thank you. I am glad I do not have to crank my car to get it started. Many men broke their arms doing that. Every now and then, when I buy a gallon of milk, I am grateful that I don't have to take a bucket on a cold morning in January and head to the barn to milk old Daisy. She had a bad habit of flopping her tail in the milk bucket and then winding her tail right around my face.

But some things were good about the "good ole days." Except for the Hollywood crowd and a few exceptions, people got married for keeps. Divorce was not the norm. I don't ever remember hearing any of my school mates discuss the perils of step-mothers or step-fathers. If unmarried people lived together, it was called "shacking up" and was looked down on. Now and then, a girl would get pregnant out of wedlock, but it was not celebrated.

Homosexuals were called "queers" and did not carry picket signs to tell the world. Abortions were rare. Marriage was considered honorable. If people took out bankruptcy, they still thought they owed the money. Financial arrangements were often made with a handshake. My father was able to borrow on that basis and he always paid what he owed. When times were hard, I was with him one time at a clothing store in Hopewell when my Daddy paid Mr. Marks fifty cents on his account and told him he was sorry he could not pay more, but that was the best he could do right then. Mr. Marks said, "That's all right, J. W., I know you are good for it. Do you need anything else for you or the family?" People learned how to "make do" as my mother often said. We bought flour

No. 2826 B Hopewell, Va., 4 - 19 194 7

Received of *J. W. Adams*

The sum of $ 2 00 on account.

MARKS CLOTHING CO.

SAVE YOUR RECEIPTS   By *Le*

Clothing store receipt (1947).

and some animal feed in sacks with various patterns. My mother would wash these and make shirts for us. We were not too proud to wear them. I grew up in a family which appreciated little things. When I was a child, I would save up nickels and dimes and with $2 or $3 dollars, buy a small gift for everyone in the family at Christmas time. Of course, money went farther then than it does now. My Grandmammy would help me wrap these gifts for Christmas. Once I bought my mother a long handled fork to use in the kitchen. While Grandmammy was trying to figure out how we were going to wrap it, she said, "Son, I hope you don't ever save up enough money to buy your Daddy a new pitchfork." While there are some things I am glad to be without from those days, I would not trade my treasure house of memories for all the money in the world. I truly feel sorry for children these days who grow up without learning the dignity of work, how to appreciate sacrifices made for them, and who need three hours to unwrap all their gifts and then ask, "Is that all?"

Changes in the Church

Since it first began, the church of our Lord has faced many issues. Some of these have been of minor importance while others have fractured fellowship and spawned various sects. At the time I was born, most churches of Christ met in modest buildings often in the less fashionable part of town. Many of the rural churches did not have a full time preacher and might have preaching once or twice a month. Gospel meetings were much longer than now and were highly anticipated. It was rare for a meeting to end without several people obeying the gospel. There were places where churches had very fine buildings, were well located, and where ambitious programs of work were carried on. In the late 1930's and 40's, you could travel across the country and whenever you found a congregation of the Lord's people, you would hear the same kind of preaching and observe the same things being done in worship. That began to change in some places in the late 1940's and 1950's.

A spirit of pride set in and an increasing number of members hungered for their place in the sun among the various churches. I remember in the early 1950's hearing one sister say, "I will be glad when we can build a sanctuary which will be the envy of every church in town." Speakers for meetings were sought who had academic degrees and these would be included in advertisements for the meetings. They took on a sociological tone, or were sensational, to capture attention. A closer affinity developed between congregations and benevolent institutions and the colleges. College choruses began to perform in church buildings. Some elders wanted to know where prospective preachers had gone to school. Out of all that came the cry for churches to support "our orphan home," or "our college," and to initiate huge sponsoring church projects. Brethren wanted their friends to know that the "Church of Christ" had arrived and was a force to be reckoned with on the religious landscape. Along with this hunger for recognition came a corresponding loss of conviction and a willingness to compromise the faith once delivered to the saints, instead of contending for it, as Jude pleaded (Jude 3-4). Instead of debating the cause with our neighbors, some wanted to find ways to fellowship those who taught and practiced error. Some preachers joined ministerial associations. They began to participate in sunrise Easter services.

The churches that embraced the support of institutions from the church treasury and the sponsoring church projects soon began to build kitchens and fellowship halls. In time, day care services were begun. Gymnasiums appeared, at first under the name of "multi-purpose" buildings. Churches fielded softball teams in the church leagues wearing uniforms with "Church of Christ" imprinted on them. Some were uneasy and raised mild objections. Others kept moving the goal posts. They said, "If this congregation starts supporting the *Herald of Truth*, I am gone." It did, and they stayed and said, "That is what the elders decided," as if they had no part in it. Then they said, "I'll tell you right now, if they start contributing to the college, I can't take that." Well, they did, and they stayed. They moved the goal posts again. Now, we see churches like Twickenham in Huntsville, Alabama which have had rock and bluegrass concerts in their building and have played Andy Griffith shows in Bible classes, or Oakland Hills in San Antonio, Texas where Max Lucado preaches which has added instrumental music and accepts people into fellowship who have not been scripturally baptized, or Richland Hills in Ft. Worth, Texas, where Rick Atchley preaches, which has started using instrumental music. There are some who are resisting much of this and are urging the need for respect for Bible authority, such as Alan Highers, and those who write for *The Spiritual Sword*. But I fear it is too little, too late.

Meanwhile, among churches which resisted institutionalism, the winds of change have also been blowing. There has been a softening in preaching on marriage, divorce, and remarriage. Much of this dates to the fact that a beloved brother, Homer Hailey, in the late 1980's began to publicly advocate what before he said he had held as a private opinion. His view was that the alien sinner is not amenable to the law of Christ on this subject until after he obeys the gospel. That means that a man married ten times, keeps wife number ten after he is baptized. His position nullifies the Great Commission which charges disciples to teach in all the world the gospel to every creature. If he is not subject to it, what is the use in teaching him? It also robs repentance of its fruit. Repentance demands a change of heart followed by a change in conduct. Certainly God will forgive the penitent, but he has to quit whatever he is doing which is sinful. I wrote an editorial in *Searching The Scriptures* entitled "And Wash Away Thy Wives" in which I showed that baptism does not sanctify unholy relationships. Brother Hailey had taught Bible at Florida College for many years (and at Abilene Christian College before that). He was loved and respected by a host of brethren. When I was a student at Florida College, I took several Bible classes taught by brother Hailey and had great love and respect for him. One day, at his home, I asked him what he believed on Matthew 19:9. At that time, divorce was not the problem in society it later became and it certainly was seldom found among Christians. His reply was that most of the brethren did not agree with him and that he was not on a soap box about it over the country, but that when someone asked him what he believed, as I had done, he would state his view. He indicated that this was a private opinion with him. After he explained what he believed about it, I told him that sounded strange to me and he dismissed it to the effect that I was in good company since most brethren did not agree with him. It was on that basis that I thought I could have fellowship with brother Hailey. But when it became evident to me that he was publicly teaching this, it left me, and others, with no choice but to oppose it and him. After his meeting at El Cajon, California and then a few months later at Belen, New Mexico in which he clearly advocated this doctrine (the meeting at Belen was both audio and video recorded), several reviews were published dealing with this position. These reviews were respectful of brother Hailey personally while disavowing his teaching on this subject.

The plot thickened when Ed Harrell, one of the editors of *Christianity Magazine*, wrote an article entitled "Homer Hailey: False Teacher?" In that editorial he charged that some brethren had launched an "unheroic attack on an 85 year old warrior." That watershed article was followed by a series of sixteen articles on "The Bounds of Christian Unity." In that series, brother Harrell (who is an eminent historian) questioned whether the subject "lacked clarity" and sought to include brother Hailey's position in the principles of Romans 14. His writings on that subject left the door open for the conclusion that how we determine fellowship is not so clear after all. Some younger admirers began to raise questions about a number of doctrinal points under the question, "Is that a salvation issue?" Thus the lines between truth and error became fuzzy and the area of "grey things" became enlarged. Friends and former colleagues of brother Hailey came to his defense while denying that they agreed with him. Later, brother Hailey took the same position on eternal punishment which Edward Fudge advanced in his book, *The Fire That Consumes*. There is no doubt that in his last years, brother Hailey was influenced by Edward Fudge and F. LaGard Smith on this subject. If any of those who made excuses for brother Hailey have written anything to oppose his error and his book on eternal punishment, it has escaped me.

The move toward "positive preaching" which was popularized by *Christianity Magazine* has had its effect upon many preachers and churches. The negative effect of the "positive" approach has been the creation of an estrangement between men who formerly were close personally and who worked together harmoniously for the Lord. Because of this, some men are no longer welcome where they formerly worked. It has been sad, in my last years, to see doors closed and friendships strained, if not severed. What is even worse has been to see the deterioration in the quality of preaching and teaching being done which inevitably weakens churches. Many are totally oblivious to this shift. Substantive gospel preaching has been replaced, in many quarters, by short, entertaining story telling which tugs at the heart strings but does not build strong, lasting faith. Meetings have become shorter and shorter. Exposure of sin and error has become rare. Members are thinking and dressing like the unrestrained world with very little, if anything, said to correct it. Exposure of denominational error is taboo. We must not be perceived as "fighters." Years ago, during a meeting in New Jersey in which eight people were baptized (half of them coming out of denominational churches), a brother took me aside to give me some advice. I had preached on the gospel plan of salvation and contrasted it to denominational plans, and he thought I was too hard. He said, "You know, you can catch more flies with honey than you can with vinegar." I thanked him and said, "If I ever go into the fly catching business, I'll try to remember that." Folks, we are not trying to "catch" anything. We are trying to teach people the truth and help them go to heaven and escape eternal hell.

It has been encouraging to me, on the other hand, to see increased interest in evangelism in various parts of the world. Many brethren have been generous in sending and supporting men to go to various countries and preach and have opened their hearts and their wallets to meet emergency situations when brethren in distant places suffer need. The church at Hebron Lane, where we attend now, has spent over 80% of its budget in evangelism for the last few years. It is a shame when churches build up huge sums of money in the treasury without any plans to use it for the furtherance of the gospel. It is not only shameful, it is sinful.

When I write about changes in the churches, I am not thinking of changes in the realm of expediency. It is not wrong to have a place to assemble. You can't assemble without some place in which to do it. It is not wrong to make it attractive. We cut the grass at home, trim the flowers and shrubs, and try to make our homes presentable. There is no excuse for brethren letting the grass grow knee deep around the building or having paint peeling from the gutters. Entryways ought to be attractive. If there is a tract rack, keep it well supplied with a good variety and change them periodically. Make classrooms cheerful and functional. Keep the baptistery clean and ready for use at any time.

Churches have provided air conditioning and good heating systems which are far superior to the funeral home fans for cooling and pot bellied stove for heating. We have changed from chalk boards and cloth charts to overhead and now to PowerPoint, in many places. These are changes all right, but they involve the realm of expediency. Many congregations have web sites on which to further spread the gospel. Good sound systems have helped to save the voices of preachers who used to develop huskiness from years of trying to be heard, sometimes in large buildings. It used to be thought essential for a man to succeed as a preacher, to have a strong, resonant voice. A good microphone is a welcome change. Today we have available a wide assortment of good teaching material. It has not always been that way. Yet, in days gone by, dedicated teachers with little help in the way of literature, were able to

Gospel preachers in the Adams family. Seated left to right: Connie, Wiley, Thomas Icard; Standing left to right: Jim Deason, Wilson Adams, Stan Adams, Arthur Adams.

impress young minds with the truths which equipped them for life and which softened their hearts to obey the gospel when they reached the age of accountability. We can have the brightest classrooms equipped with the latest technology for teaching, and the most eye catching materials to distribute, but it is still the message of the word of God which must be implanted into the hearts of our students.

I have to confess that it is much more pleasant to preach where the building is just the right temperature, where the building is equipped so as to make people comfortable, where people can adequately hear you and where brethren can supply CD's of the sermon right away, than it was to swelter in the heat of July or August, or shiver in the cold of January. I have preached in summer meetings where I would sweat out my shirt and coat (often times we would take off our coats). I preached in one winter meeting where the heating system did not work. I wore my overcoat and so did the hearers. I have preached in tent meetings where dogs would wander in and out and where bugs would swarm around the light bulb right above my head. I have swallowed a peck of bugs who thought my open mouth was an invitation to come in. I heard one preacher during a tent meeting who swallowed a large bug. He gagged and coughed until he finally spit it out. After he gained his composure he said, "Well, I met a stranger and took him in, but he was lukewarm, so I spewed him out of my mouth." But you know, I would gladly go back to the inconveniences of fifty years ago preaching in tents, or store fronts, or little frame buildings out in the country, and would contend with flies and bugs, heat and cold, if we could have brethren treat gospel meetings as special events and would bring their families and friends to hear the gospel ring out, and to join in singing the old songs of Zion, all to the saving of souls. Yes sir, I would trade all of our modern advancements for receptive hearts to the word. You see, what the world needs most is not a soft pew in an air conditioned edifice, with the latest equipment in sound and visual aids, but that same gospel message which Christ sent the apostles out to preach in all the world. Several years ago Foy L. Smith wrote the following:

> Brother, roll up your sleeves and thunder forth that message that rocked the hills and vales around the Jordan long ago—that pierced the hearts and convicted thousands on the day of Pentecost and subsequent days—that vibrated through the hills and valleys of Kentucky and Ohio in the days of the restoration, and that still thrills and influences the hearts of men when it is given its rightful place and emphasis! Preach it because you can do nothing greater. Preach it because you love it. Preach it because you are afraid not to preach it. And preach it exactly as it is written, neither fearing nor favoring men. Preach it every time you go into the pulpit like that time will be your last time. Preach it as "a dying man to dying men" (*Firm Foundation*, Vol. 80, Num. 5).

What Has Not Changed

It is a long time from 1930 to the present. Governments have changed, customs and transportation have changed, technology has vastly changed, and men have changed in wavering and wandering from the truth. But some things have not and will not change. Sin still separates man from God (Isa. 59:1-2). In that condition he is lost (2 Cor. 4:3-4). His destiny is eternal punishment with the Devil and his angels (Matt. 25:41, 46). But God still loves him (John 3:16). Christ died for the ungodly (Rom. 5:8). The gospel is still "the power of God unto salvation" (Rom.1:16). It is still a fact that "He that believeth and is baptized shall be saved, but he that believeth not shall be damned" (Mark 16:16). It is still true that those saved from past sin by the gospel are "to grow in grace and knowledge of the Lord and Savior Jesus Christ" (2 Pet. 3:18). It is still true that Christians are to "love not the world, nor the things that are in the world" (1 John 2:15). It is still true that those who practice the "works of the flesh . . . shall not inherit the kingdom of God" (Gal. 5:19-21). It is still true that heaven awaits the faithful (Matt. 25:46) and is more beautiful than tongue can tell

(Rev. 21:1-4; 22:1-5). And it is still true that hell is horrible beyond human utterance (Mark 9:43-48). Decades and centuries may pass, the winds of change may blow, but these truths have been my compass through the shifting scenes of nearly seven decades. I plan to cling to them the rest of the way.

Chapter 16

Toward The Sunset

The preacher wrote, "To every thing there is a season, and a time to every purpose under the heaven: a time to be born, and a time to die"(Eccl. 3:1-2). The Hebrew writer said, "And it is appointed unto man once to die, but after that the judgment" (Heb. 9:27). "For a thousand years in thy sight are but as yesterday when it is past, and as a watch in the night. . . . The days of our years are threescore years and ten; and if by reason of strength they be fourscore years, yet is their strength labor and sorrow; for it is soon cut off, and we fly away. . . . So teach us to number our days, that we may apply our hearts unto wisdom" (Psa. 90:4, 10, 12).

Sometimes I am shocked when I look in the mirror and wonder, "Who is that old man I see?" The one with sparse but grey hair and with bags under his eyes. Time and age take their toll. I was made to realize that six years ago when I was shooting basketball with a grand daughter who was then fifteen years old. I jumped up to put back a missed shot and suddenly found myself on the ground. At the time I thought only my pride was hurt, but later had to have surgery to repair a torn ligament. I am now retired from basketball. Bobby and I have tried to take care of ourselves physically. We both have a twenty minute routine of exercises which we faithfully do every morning when we first arise. We try to walk thirty minutes a day, outside, when the weather permits but on a treadmill when it is not so good. When we are in meetings, we have often walked in malls when one was nearby. We both enjoy walking on trails in parks. We try to eat sensibly and take our share of vitamins. But the clock is still ticking and days of youth are over.

A number of friends have asked, "When are you going to retire?" My response is always the same. "I'll rest when I get to heaven." How long a man should continue to preach depends on several things. The work of some has been cut short by failing health. I attended the funeral of James P. Miller who died at age sixty-two. Franklin T. Puckett left us at age sixty-six. W. W. Otey lived well into his nineties. I know several men who had to sit on a stool to preach, but they kept on as long as they could. Sometimes, as a man ages, he tends to become bitter over some things which have happened to him which disappointed or discouraged him. Some men, who have dedicated their lives to the cause, are neglected or mistreated in their declining years. Some tend to second guess the work of younger men who are called on to do what they once did. Sometimes older men weaken the impact of their life's work by foolish choices and by taking positions which they would have rejected in younger years. Sometimes a man's mind begins to slip without his realizing it. I have heard men well into their 80's whose minds were sharp and whose material was well organized and presented with clarity and force. I have heard others who had a tendency to ramble and spend too much time reminiscing. I have heard some men try to preach who were in the early stages of Alzheimers disease. Sometimes a man just needs to vacate the pulpit and leave that work in younger hands. I have asked my family to keep watch and if they think I am more a hindrance to the work of preaching, than a help, to please tell me. I hope they will do it gently. I am not sure how I will react, but I do not want to be a hindrance to the work to which I have devoted most of my life.

As a preacher grows older, he has to contend with the encroachments of age but he also has to face the fact that sometimes brethren need and want the services of younger men. It is easy to understand that when you are a younger man, but not so easy when you get older. My meeting schedule used to stay full five years in advance. Then it dropped to three years, then two, and now it is from year to year. I am well aware that the kind of preaching I do is not welcome in some places, even where I have been several times before. But I also know, that brethren have a right to call on those they believe are best equipped to provide the help they need at the time. I wrote an article once in *Searching The Scriptures* entitled "Book 'Em" in which I urged brethren to include younger men in their meeting schedules. So, I have no right to complain if brethren do that very thing. My younger days were blessed by the helping hands extended to me by older Christians, and especially older preachers. I have really tried hard to be a friend to younger men for I know how much that means.

Life does not always turn out the way we plan it. If I had my way, I would die with my boots on, either in the pulpit or just after preaching, or else on the trail there or returning home from preaching some place. But I may end up totally incapacitated and dependent on others for daily survival. I would like to be able to take care of Bobby as she ages and her health fails. But she wants to do the same for me. Something will have to give somewhere. Eight years ago, we sold our home at Brooks where I had lived for twenty-eight years. Our children and grandchildren had many memories there and did not want to see us sell it. Some of the grandchildren pleaded with us not to sell it. We had one and a half acres with the house plus a wooded lot behind it with another acre and a half. It was hard to keep up with yard work and be gone as much as our schedule required. We had to hire someone to keep the grass cut. The house was two stories and with a full basement. It was becoming a burden for Bobby to manage. We bought a "patio home" in a development with ninety-two units. We have a yard and our house is attached to another one, but the two are separated by two double car garages which provide a nice buffer and privacy. We have plenty of living space. I took one bedroom for a study. We had a 14x16 sunroom built on the back which provides extra living space.

When some of the children asked if this was a very good idea, I told them we wanted to be independent as long as possible and besides, this way, we would not have to come and live with them quite as soon! They said, "You know, Dad, it sounds like a really good idea!" We pay a monthly fee which includes yard work, snow removal, trash pickup, and all exterior maintenance on the house. The fee is less than we were paying at Brooks for yard work and for trash pickup. We can lock it up and go to our meetings, or wherever we have to go, and not worry about it. Neither of us wants to live with any of our children. It is not best for them or for us. But I do not believe they would neglect us in time of need.

Macular degeneration has robbed Bobby of sight in her left eye, all except some peripheral vision. Two years ago, I lost sight in my right eye except peripheral sight. That has called for adjustments for both of us. She does not drive at night any more and I try to limit it for me as well. A fairly recent medication has, so far, not only helped maintain her vision in her right eye, but has actually improved it. My left eye is good. Sometimes I have a little trouble reading in pulpits where the light is not good. Reading glasses help, but they also hinder eye contact. I do not preach much from notes and that helps. I am thankful that year ago I had teachers who led me to do a great deal of memory work in the Scriptures. That has been a great blessing.

Travel Plans

We do not travel the same way we did in younger years. Since 1975, I have preached in meetings from the first of March to the end of November, usually two meetings a month and sometimes three. We have made several trips overseas to preach. So, we are accustomed to travel. After two rounds of back surgery, plus Bobby's need to walk and exercise to control cholesterol, we stop about every 100 miles, usually at a rest stop on an interstate highway, and walk for 10-15 minutes. We have stopped in small towns near the highway at times. If we have to spend the night, or several of them, in traveling across the land, we try to get off the road before dark, find a motel, get something to eat, and then relax awhile before getting a good night's sleep. We have been blessed in that we have never had anything stolen from our car or from our room in all these years. We try to leave a small tip and a gospel tract on the pillow for the house keeper. You never know!

It is usually better for us to stay in a motel during a meeting when that is possible than in someone's home. There are several reasons for this. Most of the time, the beds are better. We have slept on beds so soft we needed to see a chiropractor for help. Or we have had them so hard it was a pleasure to get up when morning came. We have stayed in rooms so cluttered that you had no place to leave a suitcase open and not even a place to unload your pockets at night. Bobby likes to unpack her suitcase. I prefer to just open mine and live out of it. In many homes now, you are on your own about meals and it is hard to find things in someone else's kitchen. The temperature in a house has become more and more of a problem for us as we have become older. We don't feel at liberty to adjust the thermostat in someone else's home. We have nearly frozen in some places and smothered in others. After preaching at night, I need to unwind. Visiting, sometimes until late, tends to wind me up tighter so when we do go to bed, it is hard to go to sleep. Please don't misinterpret what I have said here. We have stayed in many homes over the years and have made many, many good friends. Brethren who have shared their homes and hearts with us have usually been generous and thoughtful. These are just general observations made here because numerous brethren have asked us about these things. As we grow older, new challenges greet us in traveling about for meetings.

Guessing what the weather will be at certain seasons of the year and in different places, is always problematic. We often guess wrong. We were in Denver one time in May when it snowed six inches one day. We were not prepared. One time we went to Greencastle, Indiana (where I have held six or seven meetings) in April. Bobby asked if I was going to take my overcoat. I said, "No, it's springtime and I am not going to lug along a heavy coat." "O.K.," she said.

Well, it turned cold, snowed during the week and I had to borrow an overcoat. Guess who said, "I told you so"? Other times we have taken heavy clothes and regretted it when it turned warmer than expected.

Since September 11, 2001, traveling by air has changed in many ways and poses special problems for those of us who are growing older. There are some things you need while in flight that are now restricted. Airlines have cut back on food service and many flights involve meal times. Unless you have time to buy a sandwich to take on your flight, you can have a problem, especially if you have low blood sugar, as I have had for many years. Some people do not live with much routine about meal times, or anything else. But we do. We have learned to take nuts, snack bars, or cheese crackers along just in case. Aging also creates problems about luggage. Many suitcases are on wheels now and that is a blessing, but Bobby is not supposed to lift more than thirty-five pounds because of macular degeneration. I have lingering back problems at times, all of which adds to the perils of traveling when you are getting older.

It is getting harder for us to find addresses late in the day where we are invited for meals. Street signs are not always easy to see and are not consistently located from place to place. When it starts to get dark, it is very difficult to find house numbers or numbers on a mailbox out in the country. We have been able to locate people all over the county for many years, even before Google or Mapquest, but must admit that it is becoming more difficult. We have often had folks to say, "It's easy to find, you can't miss it." Well, yes, I can and I have. By the way, we learned years ago that men usually give better directions than women. Men give you route numbers and road or street names while women want to tell you what is on all four corners where you turn, plus too many other markers before you get to that turn. And mileage from point A to point B? Sorry, ladies, that is just not your thing! But so far, we have managed to get older and still keep our appointments. How much longer that may last, is another question. That is, if we can remember where we are. On one trip across the country, we awakened one morning in a motel in Kansas (I think), and one of us asked the other, "Where are we today?"

Frustrations

One of our frustrations in growing older is not being able to spend enough time with our children and grandchildren. Between us we have eight children, thirteen grandchildren, and four great grandchildren. They are scattered around the country. As grandchildren reach a certain age, they want to go to camps, or are involved in sports and other activities. Then they get jobs and their time is even more limited. They all have their own lives and schedules to meet just as we do. But it still saddens us not to have more time with them.

The nature of our work for years had taken us away from home and, while we enjoy worshipping with brethren where we are members, we often miss meetings because we are in one ourselves at the same time. We miss many get-togethers among Christians which we would love to attend. We do not get to entertain as much as we would like. We also have to miss other meetings in the area where we live. There are only so many days and nights and we have to decide what we can and cannot do.

Thankful

We meet many people who are much younger than we are and who suffer from poor health. Many younger people marvel at the schedule we keep. We don't stop to think about it much, we have been used to it for so long. Bobby can still outwork many women who are far younger than she. She can out walk me now. While I do stretch exercises every day, she does some which would put me in the hospital if I tried them. We both love to ride horses and do so at every opportunity. When we go on a trail ride, she tells the wrangler not to give her the slowest nag in the barn, but one with a little spirit. Neither of us takes much medication. We have children who love us and friends and brethren who treat us better than we deserve. Our lot has been cast in a country which has enjoyed freedom and opportunity. It is rapidly changing from the America in which we were born and reared. But we have lived in a time when we have enjoyed material prosperity such as we could not have imagined as children. I am thankful that I will not live long enough to suffer the disadvantages of the socialistic state which we are rapidly becoming, but I regret that our children and grandchildren must learn to endure it.

I am thankful that I had godly parents who sacrificed to make life better for me than it was for them. I am thankful that they loved the Lord and taught me to love him and want to spend my life serving him. I am thankful for my siblings. My brother, Wiley, has been a hero to me all of my life. I never saw anyone sacrifice more with his family to prepare himself to preach than he did. By choice, he has labored with small churches in needy areas and even now, well into his 80's is working with meager wages to keep a light burning with a small church at Centerville, Georgia. My sister, Glenda, never caused our parents any grief. She was valedictorian of her high school graduating class. She married a good man, Thomas Icard, who became a gospel preacher and left this world at the young age of forty-nine. She has worked very hard to take care of herself

Bobby and Connie on horses in Wyoming (a favorite thing in one of our favorite places).

and is still working well past the time when many others would have retired. I am thankful for the joy of children. Wilson preaches in Murfreesboro, Tennessee and edits *Biblical Insight*. He and Julie have four children. Martin works in Washington, D.C. for the Federal Aviation Administration and serves as an elder in the church at Centreville, Virginia. He and Joanie have three daughters. Three of Bobby's sons live in Louisville, Kurt, Rick and Gordon. Gordon is mentally ill and we have our share of heartaches about him. Kurt has three step-children. Rick has one daughter. Donna, who is the oldest, lives in northern Virginia and has one daughter. Elynn and Kimberley both live and work in Orlando, Florida and worship at South Bumby Avenue. Elynn has two sons and Kimberley and Wally have a son and daughter. We love them all.

I am thankful for the godly people who have affected my life. They include numerous gospel preachers, elders, deacons, teachers, and dedicated Christians. They have encouraged me by their faithfulness, often under trying circumstances. People in the world do not understand the bond which Christians have or the joy we have in each other's company. Many mother and father figures have stood by me to teach, rebuke and encourage. There have been some who have been as close as any brother could be. People I could trust and confide in safely. All of these have made the journey not just bearable, but pleasant and often joyous.

I am thankful for the two godly women which the Lord brought into my life. Bobbie 1 stood by me in younger years, never flinched when we had hard decisions to make, urged me on in the work of preaching the gospel, gave birth to our two sons and showed true courage in the face of the illness which took her life much too soon. I am thankful that out of that sorrow and pain, the Lord brought Bobby 2 into my life to love me and to stand by my side in the work of the kingdom as we together face the sunset of our lives. Since both of us came through the valley of loss and disappointment, we know how special each day truly is. We both have our anxious concerns about those we love but she has been a rock and a refuge for me, and I have tried to be that for her. As she often says "We have our 'chothers' (contraction for 'each other,' once said by a small granddaughter)."

But above all that, I am thankful to my God who did not give up on me but who, out of pure grace, rich mercy, and inexplicable love, sent His only Son to earth to offer Himself as a sacrifice on the cross of Calvary, so I might be forgiven and live with hope and the promise of eternal happiness in the world to come. I am thankful for the fact that Jesus came, that He impoverished Himself so that I might be rich, and that He suffered the shame and agony of the cross for my sins. I expect to meet Him and thank Him personally. Paul said, "When Jesus, who is our life, shall appear, then shall we also appear with him in glory" (Col. 3:4). I am thankful for the grand work of the Holy Spirit in revealing the truth of the gospel to the apostles and prophets so I could know what the mind of God is and what He expects of me.

Every day draws us nearer the setting sun. How much longer it will be, mercifully, we do not know. If I could start all over, I would choose to spend my life as I have, in preaching the gospel. I hope there will be some in heaven because we taught them the truth. If I could start over, I would still choose both Bobbie 1 and Bobby 2 to make the journey with me at the same points in life when that choice was made. I pray for wisdom and for health of body and mind to proclaim the glad tidings with Bobby 2 at my side, until the time comes when we must unclasp our hands and one of us must go on ahead to that fair haven where no storms arise, where no fears dismay, where no sorrows ever come, and where we may rest from our labors in the eternal arms which shall ever enfold us. It has been a long time since that first sermon at Pike Road and that first meeting with the church on the nine foot road. Or has it? Where have the years gone?